MAKING ACTION TOYS IN WOOD

MAKING ACTION TOYS IN WOOD

Anthony and Judy Peduzzi

 Sterling Publishing Co., Inc. New York

The line illustrations were drawn by Ethan Danielson from the original designs supplied by Shoogly Lums Folk Toys, and the colour photographs taken by Bob Croxford

Published in 1985
by Sterling Publishing Co., Inc.
Two Park Avenue
New York, N.Y. 10016

Printed in Great Britain

Library of Congress Cataloging-in-Publication Data

Peduzzi, Anthony.
  Making action toys in wood.

  "First published in Great Britain under the title,
Making moving wooden toys" – T.p. verso.
  Includes index.
  1. Wooden toy making.   I. Peduzzi, Judy.   II. Title.
TT174.5.W6P43 1985   745.592   85-12674
ISBN 0-8069-1224-3 (pbk.)

Published by arrangement with David & Charles Ltd.
This edition available in the United States, Canada and
the Philippine Islands only.

Contents

This book is dedicated to our parents,
James and Emily Lincoln and John and Margaret Peduzzi,
with love and gratitude

I have gathered a posie of other men's flowers
And nothing but the thread that binds them is my own
Montaigne

Introduction

The appeal of creating moving folk toys is universal, transcending all barriers of age. Here, within the pages of this book, is something to suit everyone – from the youngest child, to the most sophisticated adult. Many of the toys are suitable for mentally and physically handicapped children and adults. Some can be made by children, all can be made for children as well as for grown-ups. All are adaptable as projects in schools, art and technical colleges, and craft courses, as well as gifts for various members of the family. The satisfaction to be gained by making performing toys, and in making them well, is enormous. *You* can make a plaything that is bound to evoke delight and satisfaction in the recipient – and the sheer fun of toymaking is what this book is all about!

The choice of toys presented here ranges from the very simplest to the more complex; and in order to provide more challenge and interest, we suggest alternative ideas and variations upon some of the themes. After reading this book and making the toys, you may discover ways to modify, adapt or improve them in ways to suit your particular tastes. Ingenuity and imagination can take you a long way, and it is truly marvellous just what you can achieve once you put your minds and hands to work for you!

Where possible, we provide some historical background to each toy. We had a great deal of difficulty in choosing the toys for this book, as so many entertaining and ingenious performing toys have been created down the ages, but we believe that you will be happy with these, our initial selection of moving folk toys.

To begin at the beginning
The reason that moving folk toys are so popular today is that, throughout the centuries, people have changed little – they remain fascinated, even hypnotised by colour and by movement. You have only to think of the kite, windmill, zoetrope, cinema and television, to realise the truth of this. People are as equally thrilled by moving dolls, as representations of the human figure, as they are by puppets, marionettes, clockwork clowns, robots, automata, and the eternally captivating Mr Punch. One of our friends, Professor Vernon Rose, once invited us to watch his Punch and Judy show. There, below his glowing showcase stage, sat hundreds of children of all ages, with their parents: two generations reared on watching television. And yet, within twenty seconds of the famous drama commencing, all were totally immersed in the escapades of our hero, Mr Punch. The entire audience with great gusto joined in the 'Oh, no you can't – oh, yes I can!' episodes, which goes to prove that something outstanding is always appreciated, in any age and by any age group.

Of course, the great advantage of performing folk toys is that, having created them, you can use them yourself. It's not a 'Penny to watch the Peepshow', for you can actually participate, and even expand upon your own creations.

The Tale Begins
It is certain that prehistoric man, even with his limited resources, was just as observant and curious and as creative as we are today. The superb pictures that he painted on cave walls in many parts of the world testify to

this. Paintings of animals and the rituals involved in their hunting must have appeared in the flickering glow of dancing firelight, to be truly moving, and alive.

The Egyptians, and of course the Chinese, had a good working knowledge of simple mobile toys, but it was the ancient Greeks who developed these ideas to make working automata of very sophisticated kinds, involving the principles of water power and gravity. Hero's perpetual water fountain in particular, has always fascinated me. To pass an idle hour or so just staring at the rays of 'magically' moving water can be heartily recommended. It is rather sad to admit, but no one nowadays can put a name to the individual inventors of simple moving folk toys of yesteryear. All we know is that at some time in the dim and distant past, in various parts of the world our anonymous ancestors sat and experimented with wood and thong and nails and paint. With a great deal of thought, love, ingenuity, imagination and patience, they proceeded to create these wonderful toys; simple toys, but there was sheer genius in their simplicity. How these types of toys spread from their humble beginnings in isolated and well-forested communities to every country of the world today is somewhat of a mystery. Very probably, one man (and every worthwhile adventure story in history begins this way) made a toy, and his friends wanted one, too. Enter the first toymaker. However, some of these toys were not originally made as playthings, but as set pieces in various religious rituals, and over the centuries they evolved into toys, pure and simple.

And so moving folk toys slowly but surely spread. For hundreds of years these types of folk toys were made on a small scale, by simple artisans, aided by their hard-working families. In the bleak depths of winter, they would be made, assembled and decorated, to be taken for sale to the fair, and market on feast days, from spring onwards. How very little the world has changed since then, for we still do exactly the same! Every country in Europe, back to the Middle Ages, has always held regular shows of some kind. St

Bartholomew's Fair, at Smithfield, London, was a very famous annual fair, where similar types of moving folk toys to ours were sold. By all accounts, some of these fairs must have been quite lively. Donnybrook Fair, near Dublin, in particular, was noted for its 'Bacchanalian routs and light-hearted rioting', as well as for the more usual side shows, amusements and merry-making. (A slight difference from the larger more sedate agricultural and craft shows that we often attend!)

Later, as trade between nations flourished and realising that an infinitely larger market for toys existed overseas, whole communities banded together to make even greater quantities of moving toys. Many skilled toymakers formed their own guilds. Soon, whole towns – notably Nuremberg in Germany – became famous for toymaking throughout Europe. With the invention of the principle of the clockwork mechanism during the fifteenth century, moving folk-toy movements and concepts were incorporated into complicated working automata (and most ingenious some of these were, too). However, these ultra-sophisticated playthings were initially made only for the wealthy folk, and it was the traditional craftsman, then as now, who carried on making the simpler, but equally effective, moving folk toys down through the years.

These folk toys enjoyed a great revival in the Victorian era (paradoxically enough, when industrial technology was at its height), and again, after World War I, when the toys were made and sold on street corners by war veterans, many of whom were disabled. These toys were then known as 'Street Toys', and also 'Penny Toys', because that is all each toy cost to buy. In World War II, when imported materials could no longer reach England, many a grandfather lovingly carved, shaped and made these playthings from the wood of old boxes and scrap timber (lumber). Even German and Italian prisoners of war held in Britain made folk toys in great quantities for British children (see Chapter 11 on Pecking Birds).

Although many moving folk toys made of plastic were imported from Japan and the Far East during the fifties, the vogue is now, as it always has been, for wooden toys, which have an aesthetic beauty all their own. We continue a long tradition, stretching back thousands of years, in the footsteps of our spiritual ancestors, and it is a proud and honourable tradition for us to be part of that great legion of moving folk-toymakers.

You don't have to be a Michelangelo

Whenever we are invited to take along our folk toys and give a lecture (or as we call it our ramblings on) to various groups of people, we can always be sure of at least two things happening at these meetings. The first is that no one is going to fall asleep when we are performing (they haven't as yet!). Secondly, we can guarantee that, during the course of the evening, one of the ladies (it is invariably a lady) will say 'My husband/grandfather/nephew/grandson/son has made one or two of these toys, but what spoils them is that we can't paint like you do.' 'Well, of course you can't', I always say. 'Everyone has their own individual style and approach to painting, 'though, you don't have to be a Michelangelo.'

I say – think back. Ignore realism, impressionism, the still-life schools, baroque art and neo-classicism, and all the rest – wonderful in their own way, but useless for our purposes. Now, look at the cave paintings of Saltadora, Spain, or the Trois Frères at Ariège, at Indian or at Eskimo art. Here you can learn something solidly useful. Here, artists succeeded in creating the purist forms of folk art, using only the bold application of a very few dexterous strokes. They managed to create wary hunters stalking their prey of bear, deer, seals and stags. This is folk art, pure and simple, and beats all your modern art.

At this point, there are usually several interruptions from the more learned in the audience, and we leave them all to it, debating the finer points of 'what constitutes effective folk art in today's world', or not, as the case may be. As we seldom understand

many of these debates, we find that this is a good time to put the glasses down on the nose, appear intelligent, and nod encouragement at any points that may be put to oneself. When everyone has quietened down again after having their say, we chip in with our ten cents' worth, and continue with the two classic examples of folk art in the twentieth century. Firstly, the brilliant cartoon films created by the late Walt Disney. Nearly two thousand skilled men and women and nigh on 200,000 separate drawings were needed to produce just one of his complete cartoon films. Look at those films closely, masterpieces such as *Cinderella, Snow White and the Seven Dwarfs, Pinocchio, Mickey Mouse* and *Donald Duck*, and you will see exquisite examples of folk art at its best. Study the expressions on the face of each character, animal as well as human. You can see clearly every range of emotion depicted – from pique to sadness, smiles, anger and ecstasy. It took the staff six months to make just one short film – but it was certainly worth waiting for! All the animation and actions here were evolved initially from just a few lines and brush strokes, and simple sketches on a drawing board.

When I was young, I was heavily influenced by Aztec art (even though I can still never quite pronounce Quetzalcoatl). When you get a chance, just take a look at the illustrated Mexican Calendar (otherwise known as the Codex Borbonicus) and you will see what I mean. The colours, shapes and settings are simply stunning. Absorb each small detail in your mind's eye, and later you may care to use bits and pieces transposed into your own work and style.

The second example of folk art that is relevant to our theme is the cartoon. I am using the word in its modern-day sense, as an amusing exaggeration of pictorial representation. Cartoons depend not upon pictorial accuracy to achieve their effect but in caricaturing the main features. And, for our purposes, we want to keep this cartoon style as simple as possible, and as happy and gay as we can. You can always develop your own style of folk art later with practice, but for now – to inspire you to start – we have put down a few simple ideas for folk toys. And a last word, regarding paintbrushes. For larger work, always buy your paintbrushes from a good artshop. For the smaller brushes that you will need, when you come to do the finer lines, it saves money if you purchase these from a toyshop. These are known as 'Children's' paintbrushes and are a lot cheaper to buy, and also last much longer. They can be narrowed to the appropriate thinness required by the judicious use of a pair of scissors.

A Little Bit of Know-How on Tools and Materials

Before you start galloping off and making the toys, I think it would be a good idea to give you a few hints and tips about tools and materials. It will make life a lot easier for you, I promise. Now, you don't have to worry. This is not going to be a chapter full of boring technical details and jargon. We have tried to make this book as interesting as possible, and easy to follow; after all, these toys are simple to make, for, didn't our own ancestors invent them and make them, using only the simplest of working tools and the trees that grew around them. They had few problems (and I like to call my problems by their right and proper name – challenges.) This makes life easier all around, and changes worry into optimism.

The first startling revelation is this one. To make the toys, you need have no knowledge whatsoever, of woodwork. All the family can make them, even the children. I will explain the mechanics and uses of the necessary tools. The tools themselves are inexpensive to buy; you may already have them around the house, or on your garage or workshop shelves, or in your handicraft or wood-working classes at school, or at college; you may have friends who are able to loan them to you, or, as a last resort, you may be able to improvise alternative tools. Tools them-selves are very important things, even the few simple tools that I will list for you here, for the very fabric of our past is split into periods where different kinds of tools were used, such as the Stone, copper, Bronze and Iron Ages. In spite of all the great modern innovations in tools of recent years, say power tools run by electricity, each fulfils exactly the same function as the tools of yore. And, as the saying goes, 'if it's good,

and has proved its worth, then you can't keep a good tool down!' The knowledge of tools and the skill in using them were, for hundreds of years, kept dead secret by the craft guilds. It is only in comparatively recent times that so much knowledge has been made available to the general public, by way of the printed word, and illustrated 'how to do it' techniques, found in many do-it-yourself books. This is how, in the main, crafts such as thatching and pottery have been kept alive, and are now thriving mightily.

Consider also that many of the tools used in specialist crafts, say even up to fifty years ago, have uses that we can only guess at in this day and age. Back in the Middle Ages, things were worse. A craft trade then was known as a 'Mystery', and all working craftsmen and indentured apprentices to a particular trade or craft were sworn to absolute secrecy. Even toymakers then were silent! And now, a professional folk toymaker speaks out, and says to you that I am here to dispel the mystique of using tools. I just want to show you all how easy it is to use simple tools to make splendid toys, without getting involved in trade tech-nicalities.

Tools

Hand Fretsaw This will be your workhorse. It is designed to cut plywood, and its deep throat allows you to cut out all kinds of shapes. The blade is fine, so that you can cut around sharp and intricate angles, and also produce interior fretwork (see fig. 2). The blade is held in place at each end by wing

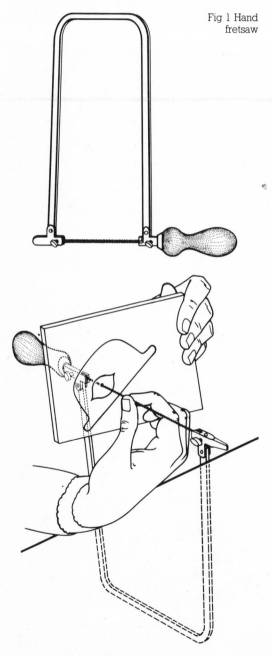

Fig 1 Hand fretsaw

Fig 2 Cutting out interior shapes

nuts. When fitting a blade, set the teeth of the blade downwards towards the handle, and saw from underneath, using a pull stroke. If you have never used a fretsaw before, don't worry. Practise on a little scrap wood first, and you will very soon get the hang of this simple hand tool.

To cut out an inside shape, drill a hole in your workpiece, then undo the wing nut at one end of the fretsaw, and release the blade. Insert the blade through the hole, then reconnect to the frame (fig. 2).

Bench V board (see fig. 3) This is a jolly handy thing to have. It's so easy to make, and makes toymaking, and cutting out, so very simple. Use any flat piece of wood with a minimum thickness of ½in, 12in×8in. Cut out a 3in wide piece at the front, to a depth of 6in, in a V shape (shown in figs. 3 and 4).

G Cramp (C Clamp) Any size will do, as long as it holds your bench V board securely to your workbench.

Hand fretsaw, bench V board and G cramp (C clamp) used together are shown in fig. 4.

Drill There is nary a toy in this book that doesn't require a drill hole of sorts. So get yourself a drill called a **twist drill**. The drill bit sizes that you will need are as follows:

⅛, ³⁄₃₂, ⁵⁄₃₂, ³⁄₁₆, ¹³⁄₆₄, ⁷⁄₃₂, ¼, ⁵⁄₁₆, ⅜, ⁷⁄₁₆, ½ (all sizes in inches)

If you are using either an electric or a hand drill, you need a drill with a ½in chuck. This is the piece that holds your drill bits to the drill.

Hammer A small cross-pein hammer is ideal. With this, you can knock in your gimp pins, use your chisel, insert dowelling, and round off rivet heads. It is also handy to have a second hammer.

Wood Chisel You need a ¼in chisel. You can trim and clear away waste wood with this. It is useful for woodcarving too.

Screwdriver Everyone's got a screwdriver!

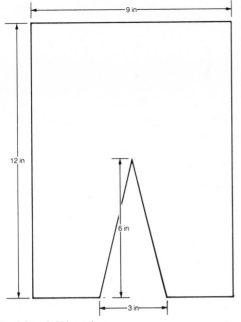

Fig 3 Bench V board

Plane Called a **smoothing plane**. Useful to chamfer the edges of the wood.

Craft Knife A handy little tool. Used in making jumping jacks etc.

Tape Rule and Flat Rule Use the tape rule for measuring length and widths of plywood; and the flat ruler for drawing straight lines.

Try Square Used for marking out, and checking that uprights of wood are square to the base. If you don't possess one of these, don't worry. Use an old hardback book instead. Stand it upright, and you will be able to see immediately if your work piece is straight, and to the correct angle.

Centre Punch This will enable you to mark the centre of the hole that you are going to drill, so that the drill bit doesn't slide away

Fig 4 Using your fretsaw with the bench V board and G cramp (C clamp)

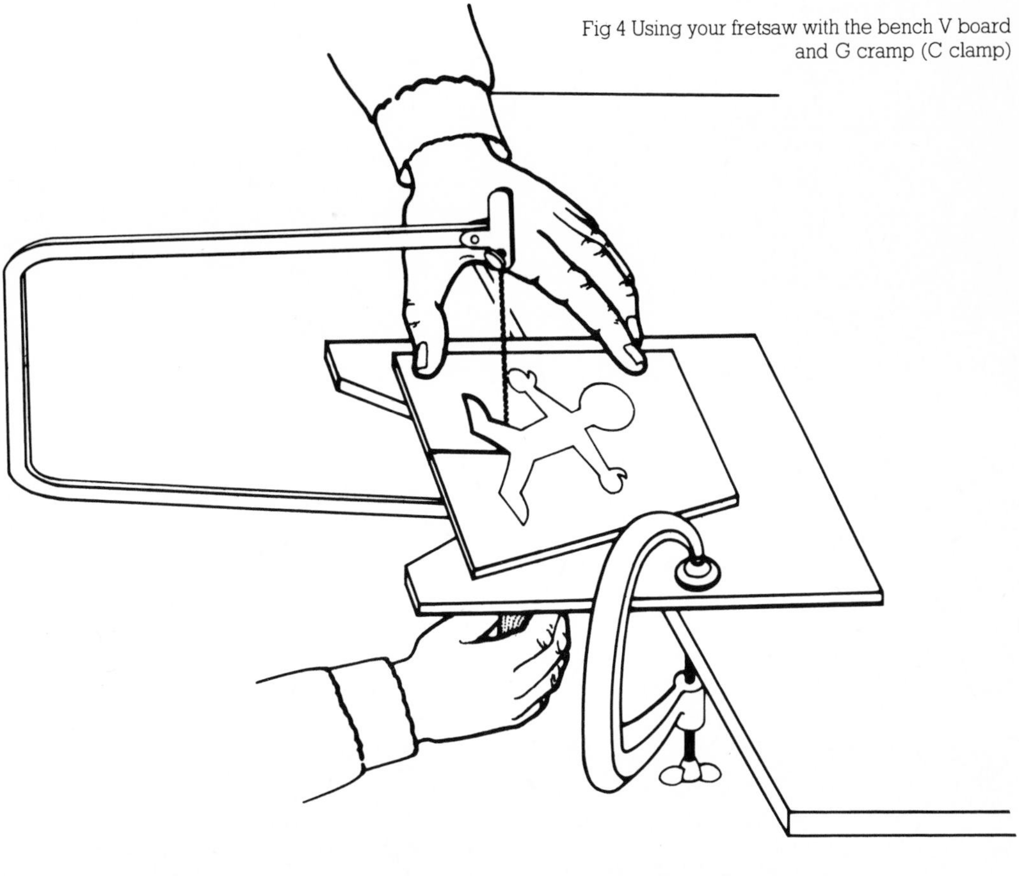

from the mark. If you haven't got one, just use a nail and hammer. Before hammering the nail or punching into the wood, lean the nail or punch slightly away from you, making sure that the point is central on the mark; then return the nail and punch to the upright position. Strike the nail or punch with your hammer. This action will ensure better accuracy.

Scissors Useful for cutting through tracing paper, cord, string or ribbon.

Pencil You will need this for each toy, so have several nearby you as you work. If you are like us, you will always seem to lose one, so have others nearby.

Pencil Sharpener As well as being indispensable for sharpening pencils, they are also superb for removing the sharp ends of dowels.

Countersunk Bit with a head diameter of ⅜in will recess a hole, and make it easier for the hole to accept a countersunk woodscrew.

Tenon Saw This is an ideal saw for cutting out small joints. It is small, easy to control and to use. If you haven't got access to one, use a **hacksaw** in its stead.

Pliers Versatile. They have side cutters to cut brass rods to length, and shape loops afterwards. They hold wooden balls when they are being drilled.

Vice (Vise) A great thing to have, as it holds things together securely. Useful when glueing wood together, and fits handily on the workbench. *Always cover the jaws of the vice (vise) when using, to prevent marking your wood.*

Files and Rasps I use wood rasps, one half round rasp and one flat rasp, which are excellent for shaping. I also find that it is handy to have a round file, commonly known as the **rat-tail** file. Combined with a half-round file, these will give your work a smoother finish.

Technical Terms Made Easy
Capping plugging a hole, usually with dowelling

Chamfer removing the edges from pieces of wood

Flush level with

Radius round off

Square to have an accurate angle

Materials
We have worked out the total materials needed to complete one of each of the toys in this book. If you wish to do so, you can now go out and bulk buy. This will save you both time and money.

Ramin Dowelling These are sold in 6ft lengths, so you will require one length of each of the following sizes, in inches: ⅛, ³⁄₁₆, ⁵⁄₁₆, ⅜, ½ and ⅝.

Wood: Ramin One six foot length of ½in × ½in.

Wood: Plywood – Birch This is strong, and has a smoothly textured surface. It is good wood for painting too. You need a piece of ⅛in thick plywood, 24in × 18in; and one piece of ¼in plywood, 26in × 48in.

Cane 16in long and ½in thick. This will be used only for the Japanese version of the acrobat on sticks.

Hardwood There are so many types of this sold throughout the world, that a comprehensive list would stretch on, almost to infinity. I use both obeche and sycamore. The best way for you to buy hardwood is to estimate your requirements, then go off to your local lumber or timber yard. Look through the off-cuts of wood there, which will be already planed and smoothed. Make an offer for the best that you can find, and ask that they be cut to the lengths you require. This will be a saving for you in financial terms.

Glasspaper Sometimes we call it **sandpaper**. This is the cheapest abrasive material available. It comes in coarse, medium and fine grades, and each sheet is approximately 11in×9in. The best grades are Fine Grade No F2, which will do admirably for rough work, and to sand away the plywood edges very quickly. Then use Fine Grade F1, for smoothing and finishing. The coarser kinds of glasspaper will leave scratches and marks and grooves in your work, so ignore these types when you come to buy any.

A good tip in using sandpaper or glasspaper on larger surfaces: cut a sheet into quarters, and use a small wooden block, say about 5in×3in×1in, and wrap a piece of glasspaper around this. When sanding, always glasspaper the wood in the direction of the grain, and not against it.

Wood Glue: PVA This comes in a small plastic container, which is equipped with a long nozzle so that you don't get wood glue spilt all over yourself.

Glue Use household glue for securing knots in the strings.

Tracing Paper You will require a good few sheets of this.

Tape or Sellotape Holds your tracing paper firmly to the plywood.

Wooden Balls You will need one ¾in ball and two 1¾in balls.

Wooden Beads You will need three ⅛in beads, one ⅜in bead and six ½in beads.

Lead Weights One ⅜in ball and one ½in ball.

String Only sold in balls, so buy a ball of string today, you will need it. Use a man-made fibre type, about 1⁄16in thick. It must be very very strong, with a high breaking strain.

Ribbons These you can buy in short lengths, in various colours. You will need 3ft of ¼in ribbon.

Cord Thin, braided, size 2H, which is equal to about ³⁄32in thickness. You will need 9ft of this. This is the type of cord used in the making of venetian blinds. We use it principally for the making of rope climbers.

Brass Rod You will need a piece 8in long and 1⁄16in thick.

Gimp Pins Small, painted nails ½in long, and 1⁄16in diameter shank and ⅛in diameter head. These are sold in small boxes.

Rivets: Copper or Brass You will want 18 flat-headed rivets ⅛in diameter, 7⁄16in long.

Springs (optional) For handicapped people. See Acrobat on Stand in the Acrobat on Sticks chapter.

Varnish Gloss varnish for the painted areas; satin varnish for plain wood.

All the above can be obtained from any good hardware store, timber or lumber yard, and art and hobby shops.

Metric Conversion Table

Nearest equivalent

Inch	mm	Inch	mm	Inch	mm
1⁄16	2	1½	38	6¾	171
⅛	3	1¾	41	7	178
³⁄32	2.5	2	51	8	203
³⁄16	5	2¼	57	8½	216
7⁄32	5.5	2½	63	9	229
¼	6	2¾	70	9½	241
5⁄16	8	3	76	10	254
⅜	10	3½	89	10½	267
7⁄16	11	3¾	95	12	305
½	12	4	102	16	407
⅝	15	4½	114	18	457
¾	18	4¾	121	24	610
⅞	22	5	127	30	762
1	25	5½	140	36	915
1¼	31	6	152	48	1220

A Little Bit of Know-How on Painting

Mankind was born with an in-built urge for immortality, a wish to continue, to be handed down, to be remembered long after death. Down the ages, man has opted for at least four different ways to achieve this goal. Then, as now, the urge to create children, to have something of oneself to see, touch and to teach and to love, and to think to oneself, there, in you, go I.

The second way is the word; to write down experiences and happenings, to show and to teach future generations. The third way is the creative urge to write and compose music. And the fourth creative urge for immortality is to draw and to paint. To depict life and laughter, and people and landscapes. The Egyptians used paints, to fabulous effect, as can be seen from their painted papyrus, coffin and stele. The Greeks transcended even these wonderful artistic achievements. Their artists were truly superb, as can be seen from painted statuette, sarcophagus, vase, amphora, cup and bowl, and water jar and fresco. And their influence in turn can clearly be seen affecting the artists of the Roman eras – in both their mosaics and wall paintings.

It is almost unbelievable, therefore, to realise that the basic ingredients used for paints for centuries were culled almost entirely from natural sources. For instance, azurite produced blue; lapis lazuli – ultra-marine; and orpiment became a yellow hue. Copper could be used for making green; the whelk for producing royal purple; malachite created another shade of green; realgar became orange; cinnabar – ver-milion; chalk was used to produce white; earths of differing hues became several shades of brown, and the humble charcoal was used in creating black colour. Even up to the nineteenth century, a mortar and pestle were required – tools for both the amateur and professional artist. And, for anyone who cannot ever remember the difference between these two, the mortar is the vessel, and the pestle is the grinding tool used to grind the raw material down to a fine powder.

However, as the age of industrialisation dawned, and with developments in both the dyeing and chemical industries rapidly expanding, things began, slowly at first, to change for the better for the artist. For instance, the colour 'mauve' could now be produced, and this was a derivative of coal tar. And as for media (now banish instantly the thought of newspaper, television and radio from your mind! In this context, we are talking of the stuffs used for mixing with paints, before daubing it on to canvas or wood), in the main, these had for centuries consisted of wax, gum, egg and oil. Various other exotic substances have also been used throughout history to produce colours. Amongst these are tree bark, cochineal and onion skins. Yes – onion skins. Apparently, when boiled, they produce a darker shade of yellow and, if you keep on boiling them, they produce brown. We only got to know about all this because we were at a show one day, and our immediate neighbour there was a professional artist. He told us that he loves to dabble and experiment with odd ingredients, including blood and bone – animal derivatives, he hastened to add! Not content to buy his paints from a good artshop, he works on his paint and colour mixing in an annexe to his studio, which, to his wife's relief she told us, is situated well away from their farmhouse home! He claims that his works are totally unique and, after seeing them, this we were very willing to believe!

Now, for painting by oil paints, tempera, gouache, watercolour and fresco, artists had been using basically the same ingredients for the past four hundred years or more. And then, dawned not the age of Aquarius, but the age of acrylics. An entirely new kind of paint. It all started in Mexico in the 1920s, where artists such as the illustrious Diego Rivera found that they had problems when they wanted to create and paint outdoor murals. He and others wanted a stable paint that would quickly dry in the local exposed conditions. They all made such a fuss about this problem that they were instrumental in bringing about a demand for such paint to be produced. And, as many discover, a demand can only be satisfied by a supply, always provided that manufacturers know of the demand. Artists as a whole are quite an insistent lot, especially when they gather together and raise their voices in harmony. And so the experimentation, discovery and, later, the manufacture of acrylic paints began. The success of this new kind of paint was astonishing, and its very success depended on just a few, but very important factors. It could easily and quickly be diluted with water; it became dry within minutes; it remained stable; it didn't alter its colour or texture and, best of all, it remained permanent. It was not until the 1950s that it was put on sale in the United States of America, and England did not see it until a few years after that. And, as a bonus, the manufacturers had somewhere along the line produced a couple of entirely new shades of colour.

Today, when you come to choose your range of colours, don't go mad and get carried away and buy dozens and dozens of kinds. Choose only, say, nigh on a dozen to begin with, and we think you will find that this choice will be entirely sufficient for your needs. After all, one of the greatest of modern painters, Mr Lowry, used only a few colours to create his great works of art. And,

don't get involved in technical details, in worries about primary and additive colours. Just buy lots of white paint – white stands out a mile, and can highlight your toys no end. Scarlet and blue, black and yellow, orange, green and purple are super choices too. White paint is also useful for mixing with the above range, on account of producing attractive pastel tones, shades and hues. Painting and colour mixing are individual choices. Don't break the bank. We will just say to you, go on, experiment with colours, and see what happens. It will surprise you when you become bold, for something fresh and new and totally good always emerges when you begin to paint. Now, you may ask, what kind of paint would you recommend using? We are not recommending any one particular paint, and the reasons are these.' There is such a huge variety of choices in each country; of acrylics, watercolours and enamels. The best thing to do is to go down to your local hardware store or quality artshop, and tell them of your requirements in full. We have always found all the staff in these types of shops most helpful. The most important thing to remember there, is not to forget to tell them that you are buying paints for use in making toys for children. Ensure that any paint or varnish that you purchase is entirely **non toxic**. Children cannot – ever – be replaced. Ensure that the paint content is also lead free, and arsenic free. (Oh yes, paint did contain both arsenic and lead.) Most countries now have strict safety regulations governing the use of paint for children's toys. However, we wish to stress that you cannot ever be too careful. Also, ensure of course that the paints of your choice are quick drying, stable and permanent.

Brushes It is here that we have to declare a personal interest. We are of the make-do-and-mend school of thought; this decrees that you do not have to spend a fortune upon brushes, as long as each is sufficiently adequate for your needs.

An artist friend has a brushbox, beautifully equipped with paintbrushes of all sizes and shapes, nestling within. These are invariably in pristine condition, with nary a speck of paint on them (quite unlike my little collection of brushes). She has Japanese bamboo brushes, squirrel and ox hair, camel hair, Chinese hog's hair brushes, and sable; and even red sable brushes which, she tells us, come from the tail hairs of the Siberian mink! I asked her once whether she had her collection of brushes insured; but all that I received in reply was a very cold stare, and then dead silence. I have just a small collection of brushes – ten to be exact – collected over the months and years. Big brushes and little brushes, and fat ones and thin ones; and all come in handy at various stages of painting. For anyone beginning, it is handy to know that brush sizes are graded according to numbers 1 to 12, and these should be sufficient for your needs. A fan brush is also useful to own. This is literally a paintbrush shaped like a fan, and as well as being useful for colour mixing, it is also just right for covering larger surfaces of wood.

Go down to your local artshop, and browse amongst the paintbrushes there. You will find something to suit your own individual needs. Pick them up, touch them, remembering that the cardinal rule is not to spend a fortune on them. From bitter experience, we have found that sometimes the most expensive brushes don't last very long. Also, look at brushes made from synthetic fibres – these are not as expensive as brushes made from natural fibres.

Now that we have sorted out paints and brushes, on to the palette for mixing the paints together. Our advice would be, don't buy one. We don't think that this is necessary. It's so much cheaper to use an old plate or saucer, and then clean it afterwards.

As for a special container in which to keep your brushes filled with water (if you choose watercolours), the best method is to use an old jar or vase, and the brushes will survive there quite happily until you need to use them next.

The last item that you will need is a soft cloth, to wipe away excess water from the bristles.

All that you basically need, therefore, is a safe and exciting range of colour paints; a safe clear varnish (don't forget to buy a separate varnish brush, obtainable from any good hardware store); a decent set of paintbrushes; a saucer; a vase; and a soft cloth.

We have now covered all the artist's equipment that you need to start you off happily painting your folk toys. The section entitled 'You don't have to be a Michelangelo' on page 9 should help to give you some confidence as an artist. We have also included in this chapter a few sketches of variations on some of our folk-toy themes that you might like to make and develop later.

Good and happy painting to you all.

1 The Whirling Whizzer

Colour plate 1

This basic toy proves what enchantment can be created from a bit of string and a piece of wood having two holes in the middle. This is one of those toys known to us as 'Haven't seen one of these for years. Used to have one as a child. Expect I can still do it. Can I have a try?' And they do – and the result is grins of delight in their prowess. And away the whole family go, walking off into the sunset, whizzers awhirl. Grandfathers, cousins, uncles and aunts and grand-children. 'Be careful not to walk into any lampposts,' we call after them.

We think it is possible that this is the oldest folk toy. I have always had the feeling that it is something Adam and Eve used to have, when things got a little dull, after Paradise. It is certainly one of the oldest musical instruments. It is probable that the whizzer was an immediate forerunner of the famous 'bullroarer'. This was a long, notched heavier piece of wood, with a cord tied to one end. When the other end of the cord was held in the hand, and the roarer whirled rapidly around overhead, then a most peculiar 'hair-raising' noise issued from its immediate vicinity. This object was also used to frighten away evil spirits.

The whirling whizzer keeps many children both busy and quiet, and it is simple to make. As a bonus, in summertime, children have told us that they can easily cut the heads off the daisies on the lawn – how's that for saving on the price of a lawn mower? People whom we have met have reminisced over whizzers that they used to own: whizzers made from buttons and cut-outs from cornflake packets; and whizzers made from cardboard milk-bottle tops, which disintegrated when wet. However, these particular whirling whizzers will not disintegrate, because they will be made from wood. The variations on this small, but effective toy, are enormous. You can make dozens of different shapes, including diamonds, squares, circles and egg shapes. You can also insert notches later to increase the musical noise content, and see what marvellous aural effects you can achieve.

Fig 1 The whirling whizzer in action

Method

This is the very first toy of the book. We have chosen this one because it is simple to make and easy to mark out. It also gives you practice in using a hand fretsaw. This whirling whizzer is a deluxe version, complete with handles, so that you will not get sore fingers from using naked strings. The shapes that we have chosen are well tried and tested. These are the 'Bow Tie' and 'S' shape patterns.

1 The whizzers shown are actual sizes, so that all you have to do is to trace around them on paper (not forgetting to mark out, absolutely accurately the two string holes). Then transfer the pattern of your choice on to your ⅛in plywood.

2 Having done this, drill your string holes, using a ³⁄₃₂in drill.

3 Now, cut out your whizzer with your hand fretsaw, making sure that you keep to the outline of the whizzer shape.

4 Glasspaper your whizzer, making certain that there are no burrs left around the edges.

5 Before painting the whizzer, check that it works properly. Thread the string through the whizzer holes, and tie a loose knot only. Then, test it out. If the whizzer is off-balance, and does not spin properly, there can be only one explanation – your holes are not drilled centrally. Reposition the holes, and redrill them. Accuracy for good working is essential to this simple toy.

6 Make the handles. Take your two pieces of 2½×⅜in dowelling. Measure from each end ¾in, and mark these four points with a pencil (see fig. 2). Then drill your four holes. These will hold your whizzer strings. Use a pencil sharpener to remove the rough edges from the dowel ends. Rub down with glasspaper, and varnish the dowels.

7 At this point, paint your whirling whizzer on both sides, using as bright a pattern as you can imagine, so that when it is set in motion the whizzer will vibrate with colour, as well as with movement and sound. For a better visual effect use a series of contrasting colours and patterns on each side.

8 To complete the assembly, start off by

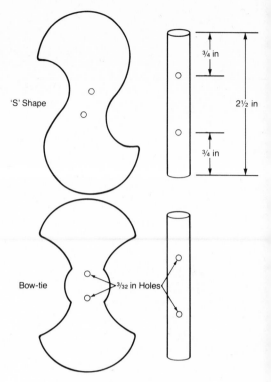

Fig 2 Whizzers and handles

'S' Shape

Bow-tie

¾ in

2½ in

¾ in

³⁄₃₂ in Holes

threading the string through one hole of the handle, then through the whizzer's first hole, and on to the first hole in the opposite handle. Back through the handle's second hole, then the whizzer's second hole, then to the second hole of the handle that you began with at first. Secure the string tightly with a strong knot.

9 You are now ready to begin whizzing! Hold the whirling whizzer as in fig 1. Then, twist your string around just a couple of times, and gently pull the strings outwards. Slowly, bring your hands slightly inwards. Allow the toy to build up the speed of the whizzer on its own volition. As momentum gathers, push and pull the strings gently. The whizzer now gathers speed and begins to whizz and to whirl. Now, you have lift-off!

Materials
1 piece ⅛in plywood, 3½in×2in
2 pieces dowelling, 2½in×⅜in
1 piece string 36in long

2 Mr Nosey the Clown
Colour plate 1

We acquired this idea from three sources. One of our friends is a woodturner, who makes the cup and ball, a toy that has been known for centuries under this name, and also another – the Bilboquet. The object of this plaything is to try and toss the ball, which is tethered to a string, into the cushion of the cup. For simple folk, such as ourselves, we found this game to be highly absorbing. Secondly, I had been reading of the life of perhaps the most talented clown and funny man of all time, Joseph Grimaldi. And thirdly, I had just watched Mr José Ferrer in the role of Cyrano de Bergerac, and had been intrigued by the length of his proboscis.

All these ideas culminated in a simple design for an intriguing toy – Mr Nosey the clown. The great advantage of this toy is that the string is attached. Unlike the game of hoopla, there is no need to stoop down to retrieve a fallen ring. Hence, this toy can be highly recommended for anyone with a bad back! Please do not be fooled into thinking that this toy is solely destined for children. We have found on our travels that there is not one adult who thinks – initially – that getting the ring on to the nose isn't going to be childishly easy. But, it is not as easy as it looks, by any means, and it becomes an interesting challenge time and time again!

Fig 1 How to work Mr Nosey

$^3/_{32}$ in Hole

Fig 2 Mr Nosey outline (actual size)

22

Method

1 Place your tracing paper on Mr Nosey (fig. 1) and draw around the outline. Then transfer your tracing on to your ¼in plywood. (If you wish, you can sellotape down the edges of your workpiece. This will prevent movement.)

2 Drill a hole in the lower end of the handle, using a ³⁄₃₂in drill, to hold the string.

3 Using your hand fretsaw, cut round the shape of Mr Nosey, making sure that you keep to the outline exactly.

4 Glasspaper Mr Nosey, making absolutely sure that there are no rough burrs on the handle. (This safeguards against splinters.)

5 And now for the ring (see fig. 2). Mark out, as described in instruction no. 1. Alternatively, you can use a pair of dividers, and mark out straight on to your ⅛in plywood.

6 Next, drill two holes, as marked out on fig. 2, using again your ³⁄₃₂in drill.

7 Using your hand fretsaw, first cut out the centre disc. To do this properly, undo the top wing nut of your fretsaw and release the blade. And now push the blade through the drill hole, as marked out on fig. 2, and refit the blade to the fretsaw. Proceed to cut out your 1in diameter hole. Release the blade and refit, and continue to cut around the outside of the ring. Just make sure that at this stage, your ring will just fit over the hat of Mr Nosey. (If it does not, then all you have to do is rub down the centre edge of the ring with glasspaper.) Remember also to allow for the thickness of the paint and the varnish. And now, glasspaper the ring.

8 Paint Mr Nosey in lovely bright colours, to make him outstanding. You can paint the figure all over, or just feature highlights such as eyes, mouth, hair and hat. The choice is yours. Then varnish the figure.

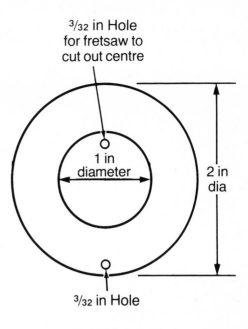

³⁄₃₂ in Hole for fretsaw to cut out centre

1 in diameter

2 in dia

³⁄₃₂ in Hole

Fig 3 Ring (actual size)

9 Assembly of this toy is simple. Using your piece of string, just thread one end through the handle, and double knot. Then thread the string through the ring, and double knot again.

Now you are ready to begin. You can make a lovely game of this, with all your friends. For instance, you can allocate five points for a ringing of the nose, ten points for achieving a hair curl, and twenty points for the hat. Then the winner can make a wotsit? stick! (See next chapter.)

Materials
1 piece ¼in plywood, 7in × 4½in
1 piece ⅛in plywood, 2⅛in square
1 piece string 16in long

23

3 The Wotsit? Stick

Colour plate 1

A kind friend brought us one of these fascinating objects which he had obtained while he was visiting Pennsylvania in the United States, where it is apparently known as a 'Whimmy Diddle'. I couldn't get it to work at all initially, but Anthony, with his infinite wisdom and patience, had it working within a couple of minutes. Soon he had produced a far better version that worked so much more easily for all age groups. Still, the thing had me baffled. How did it work? Why did the propellor change direction upon command? A five-year-old boy showed me how to do it in the end. I felt such a fool, that is, until we went out to sell the toy, when I discovered that a great number of well-educated adults of both sexes could not make it work either, until they were shown the way!

A most amusing story that we heard about the wotsit? stick came from a customer of ours, who had previously bought one of these toys. A commercial traveller in the microchip industry, he travels the world regularly and extensively on behalf of his company. He returned to us to buy a dozen more sticks for all his friends, as the initial purchase had given him so much pleasure. 'I took the wotsit? stick to my local golf club, and showed it off to the chaps there, who were all vastly amused by it. One of the members is the club bore, a particularly pompous airline pilot. "Oh, I can do that easily", he says. "Okay mate", I said, passing it over to him, "fly that!" Ten minutes later, he is still struggling to make it move, even one way; and five minutes after that, he throws it down in disgust; shouts "rubbish", and storms out, much to everyone's delight.'

Well, we may make rubbish (we have never denied it!), but at least it is interesting rubbish. And a vast number of people, year after year, come back to tell us how much pleasure all the various members of their families have derived from just one little stick!

The workings baffle all age groups initially, for a very short time, but, when discovered, provide a gorgeous plaything for both young and old. We later found out that this toy is well known in different parts of the world, including Australasia. It is called many different names – and used to be sold in England, in the aftermath of World War I, as a 'Penny Toy', by street traders. We called it our wotsit? stick, because so many people said to us – 'What's it do?'

So we show them. And rub our little sticks upon the notches, so that the propeller revolves one way. Then shout 'Abracadabra!' as the propeller commences to turn in the opposite direction, without pausing.

Plate 1   Clockwise from top left: Foot Clappers (page 32); the Wotsit? Stick (page 24); Mr Nosey, the Clown (page 21); Whirling Whizzers (page 19)

Plate 2   Clockwise from top: the Rope Climber (page 35); the Polly Parrot Tumbler (page 48); the Balancing Parrot (page 50)

Plate 3   Jumping Jacks: Humpty Dumpty (page 39); Clown (page 39); the Bowler Hat that Winks (page 39)

Plate 4   Acrobats: (left) on Bars (page 57); (right) on a Stand (page 57); (front) on Sticks (page 57)

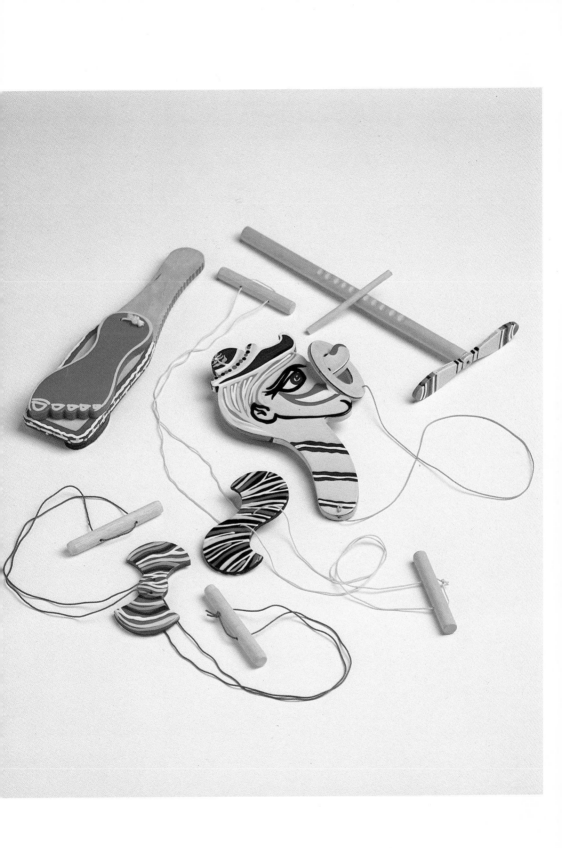

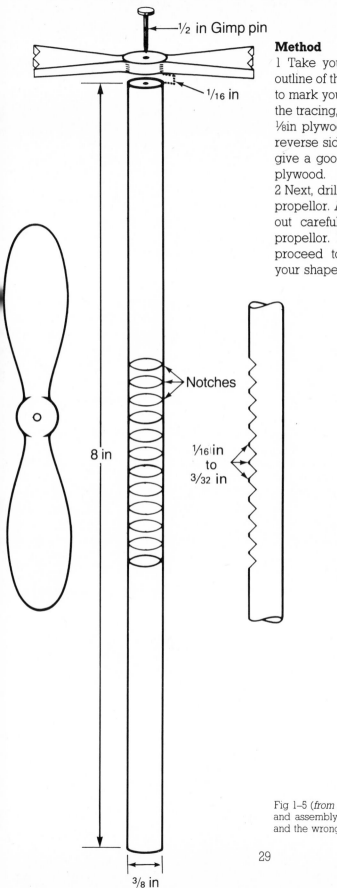

← $\frac{1}{2}$ in Gimp pin

$\frac{1}{16}$ in

8 in

Notches

$\frac{1}{16}$ in
to
$\frac{3}{32}$ in

$\frac{3}{8}$ in

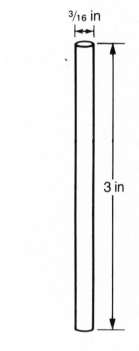

$\frac{3}{16}$ in

3 in

Method

1 Take your tracing paper, and trace the outline of the propellor (fig. 1), not forgetting to mark your centre hole. Do not cut around the tracing, just transfer it straight on to your ⅛in plywood, but remember to pencil the reverse side of your tracing paper, so as to give a good clear outline on your piece of plywood.

2 Next, drill a hole for your gimp pin, in your propellor. And, using your hand fretsaw, cut out carefully around the outline of your propellor. Having done this, you can then proceed to glasspaper over and around your shape.

Fig 1–5 (*from left to right*) Propeller (actual size); Stick and assembly; The right way to cut the notches . . . and the wrong way; Rubbing stick

29

3 Now for the stick (see fig. 2). To cut out the notches along the stick is simple; there are no set measurements here. The object is to achieve a good vibrating sound, because it is this – together with the action of your fingers, and that of the smaller stick – that causes the propellor to rotate. There are two ways of making notches. Firstly, you can use your hand fretsaw, tenon saw or hacksaw to make the cuts. Secondly, you can use a square file, or even a round file. Do not cut too deeply, about a depth of from $\frac{1}{16}$in to $\frac{3}{32}$in is sufficient. This would represent one stroke of your square file (see fig. 3). Keep your notches in a dead straight line, as shown in fig. 2. Avoid results as shown in fig. 4 – if you have done this, have you got problems! Start again.

4 Having completed this task successfully, use a pencil sharpener to remove any rough edges from the stick ends, and also the rubbing stick (see fig. 5). Now give them both a good glasspapering to make them as smooth as possible.

5 Before assembly, paint the wotsit? stick propellor with bright, bold lines. When this begins to spin you will want the propellor to stand out, like a lighthouse on a dark night. Paint both sides, and then varnish the propellor.

6 This is an easy toy to assemble. Using your gimp pin, nail the propellor to the stick, ensuring that it falls dead centre of the stick end. Lightly tap in your nail, but not too deeply as you will want a $\frac{1}{16}$in clearance between propellor and stick end. If you push the nail in too far, you will rub and rub your stick, and won't ever achieve lift-off. Look at the assembly of the wotsit? stick (fig. 2).

Special note Do not use brass or copper nails for this project, as the wotsit? stick will not rotate. For your next project try to discover why not – the answer makes fascinating exploration into the realms of physics and the laws of momentum, vibration and resonance, and also the properties of various types of metals.

Now that you have assembled your wotsit? stick, we imagine you standing with it in your hand, and wondering what to do next! First, take a look at fig. 6. Copy the action, hooking your index finger around the left-hand side. Hold your rubbing stick on top of the notches, in the position shown in the drawing. All you have to do now is to slide your finger and rubbing stick both backwards towards you then forwards. Continue doing this to produce the vibrations necessary to start your propellor working, clockwise. Now, slide the rubbing stick across the larger stick, meanwhile removing your index finger. Then, place your thumb end on the right hand side of the stick (this position is shown in fig. 7). Rub your smaller stick as before, up and down the notches, and the propellor will first halt, and then commence to rotate in an anti-clockwise direction. Easy, isn't it, and just pure magic.

If you are ambidextrous, you will have no problem, but if you are left-handed, reverse the instructions just given, and you too can enjoy mastering the wotsit? stick. And always remember – practice makes perfect!

It is possible to substitute whizzer shapes for propellor heads for the wotsit? stick. And, of course, sooner or later, you are going to experiment and try all manner of alternative shapes and sizes of propellors.

Warning Do not make your wotsit? stick too large, and do not try it outdoors on a windy day. If you do, you may find yourself wrongly identified as a UFO.

Materials
1 piece dowelling, 8in × $\frac{3}{8}$in
1 piece dowelling, 3in × $\frac{3}{16}$in
1 piece $\frac{1}{8}$in plywood, 3$\frac{1}{2}$in × 1in
one $\frac{1}{2}$in gimp pin

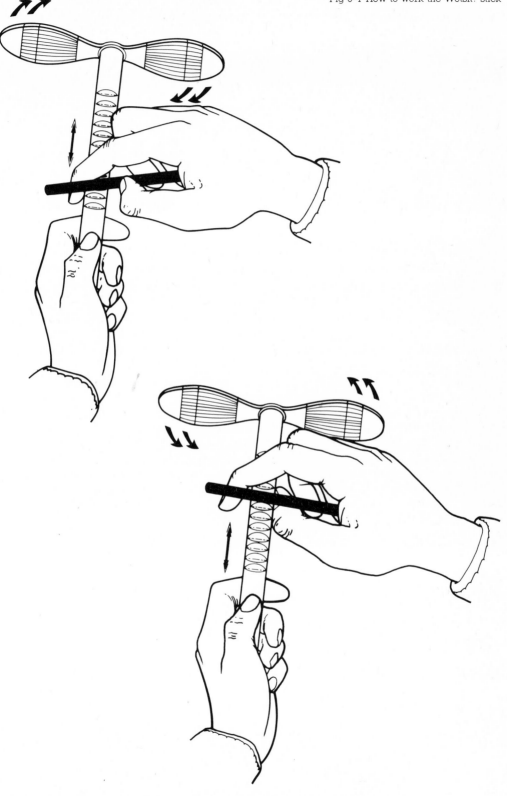

Fig 6–7 How to work the Wotsit? stick

4 The Foot Clappers
Colour plate 1

The clappers were one of the earliest folk toys that we made. 'Do you think anyone will want them?', I asked Anthony wistfully. 'They're awfully loud.' I needn't have worried. They were, and still are, an instant success. One of the oldest, simplest and most versatile toys in history the clappers probably evolved along with one of the earliest musical instruments known to man – the 'bones'. These were two bones shaped into matching flat parallel oblongs and held in one hand between the fingers, and knocked together to create rhythm.

The ancient Egyptians used the clappers, not only to scare away locusts from their growing crops, but also to ward off demons and evil spirits at religious ceremonies devoted to their gods. They were shaped then, not as feet, but as hands, and elaborately decorated with signs and symbols representing words of great power. Anthony had the idea of making them shaped as feet, after visiting his chiropodist. Musicians, especially folk musicians, have used these for centuries, with great effect, down to the present day, to complement the sounds of both whistles and snare drums. They were used by jesters in the courts of Europe in the Middle Ages to gain attention when they wished to crack a joke. In World War I, clappers were issued to air-raid wardens in England, to give the population advance warnings of Zeppelin air attacks.

As well as being primarily a simple percussion instrument, or simple rattle for a child, many of our customers for these toys have told us of the uses to which they have been put. Reasons for purchase ranged both far and wide. One lady uses them to summon her husband when she requires breakfast in bed; they were used for obtaining quick service at a slow-serviced restaurant; they were taken on holiday to Spain to use as maracas. A large number of grandmothers freely admitted to buying them to send to their daughters-in-law's children, all of whom resided in either a part of the country far away from themselves, or in another land altogether. However, our very favourite reason is buying them for lost children, and the reason for this is that aforementioned children do not stay lost for very long with one of these toys clasped tightly in their chubby little fists! On a serious note, if there is a bed-bound person in the house the clappers are invaluable should swift attention be required at short notice. Also, they are very popular with handicapped children, who can and do make up their own words, patterns, songs and rhythms to accompany the sound of this toy. A tip if you want to make softer-sounding clappers. Just bind the cord that holds the feet together a little more tightly, and then they will not emit as much noise as they do normally.

Various shapes, apart from feet, can be constructed, for instance, hands. The simplest way to make these is to draw around your own hand's shape, then transfer the pattern on to wood and cut out two matching pieces. You can choose to have either a closed hand or an open one with fingers outspread. Then you may wish to graduate to making birds, then clapping dolls and animals of all kinds. The world is yours with a clapper!

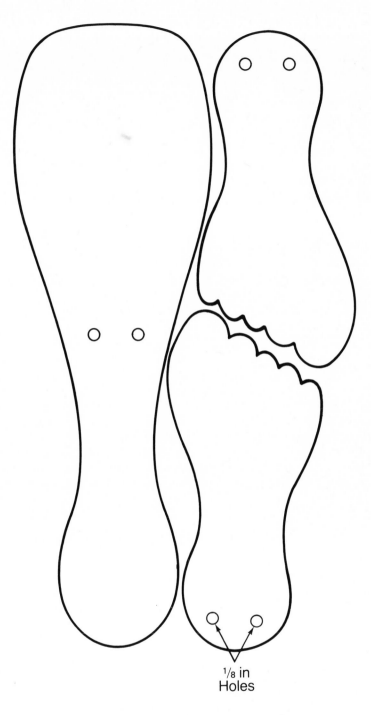

$^1/_8$ in
Holes

Fig 1 Foot clappers (actual size)

Method

1 Once again, we take our tracing paper and draw the outline of our pattern round both feet and the one handle. Do not omit to mark the string holes (fig. 1). This pattern can be cut to the same size as your plywood piece. Pencil the reverse of your tracing paper and then transfer the outlines to your piece of plywood. To keep it steady, tape down with sellotape.

2 Drill the holes for the string, using an ⅛in drill. Now cut out, using your hand fretsaw, keeping to the line. We emphasize these points now because, later in the book, you will need to be fairly accurate; and so, starting with the easy toys, this will give you plenty of practice. Now that you have your pieces cut out, give them a good glass-papering, again paying special attention to the handle (we don't want any little 'uns getting splinters; or big 'uns, if it comes to that).

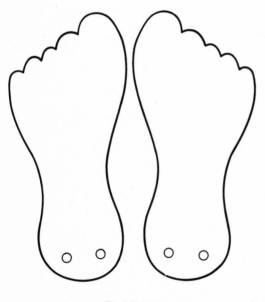

Fig 2 Painting

3 Now for the painting. Firstly, place the feet on a board, big toe to big toe, as shown in fig. 2. Paint them a bright colour, not forgetting to outline the toenails. Paint only one side of the clappers because, if you paint both sides, the clapping sound is considerably reduced. When they are completely dry, you can then varnish both sides of the feet and also the handle.

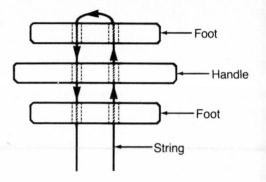

Fig 3 Threading the parts together

4 To assemble, all you have to do is to thread the parts together (see fig. 3). Take one end of your string, and thread it through one hole in your first foot, then through one of the holes in the handle and through the hole in the second foot. Reverse the procedure, coming back through the remaining holes. Now tie a triple knot, and finally, don't forget to glue the knots – this will make the feet more secure.

If you want them to sound more loudly, just hold one foot by the toes and pull it back slightly, and this will stretch the string. To test out the foot clapper we would recommend that you do not (if you happen to live in a residential zone) take it out at midnight (even if there is no moon). If you did, however, you would soon learn just how quickly sound can travel across a great distance. If, however, you have ambitions to be a busker or hustler, then there is nothing more effective at quickly attracting the attention of a passing crowd.

Materials
1 piece ¼in plywood, 6¾in × 3¾in
1 piece strong string 6in long

5 The Rope Climber
Colour plate 2

This toy has a particularly nautical history. We have been told, by many people, that on the old sailing ships the sailors used to carve and make these toys to while away the time on long sea voyages, and present them to their children when at last they reached their home port. The designs then involved two main characters. One was a sailor and the other a monkey, and the name given to this toy then was 'Admiral up a Mast'. A naval historian of our acquaintance has pointed out to us that this was a double jest of a rather bitter nature. We know that 'climbing the rigging', let alone the mast was one of the most dangerous and gruelling tasks that sailors were obliged to undertake. And we were also given to understand that in those days very few admirals went remotely near, let alone up, the mast. So, to name this toy thus, speaks volumes for the seafaring life of those days. It is, however, heartening to know that sailors then, as now, maintained a great sense of humour.

We named the toy 'The rope climber – alias Nicholas's favourite', because it is. Sharing a craft marquee at a big show once were Dave and Kathy, who are potters and Nick's parents. Nicholas himself at that time was just under two years of age, a bright and handsome boy with the most appealing eyes. He was very happy to help us demonstrate the toys, but became particularly fixated upon the rope climber. He could work it a treat, and spent the days showing its workings to everyone in sight, and advising them to have one! He became so enthusiastic about its merits, that he even brought his milk and cookies to the stall, and deposited them beneath the demonstration rope climber that we always keep at the front of the stall. Together with these endearing traits, and his own brand of patter, he had most everyone in tears of amusement. In honour of his being our youngest and most successful salesman, we called the toy 'alias Nicholas's favourite'!

Method

1 Take your tracing paper and trace the outline of Humpty Dumpty (fig. 1). After the pencilling of the reverse side, and sellotaping the pattern to your piece of plywood, you can now transfer the outline to your workpiece.

2 Cut out, using your hand fretsaw, keeping to the lines, and then glasspaper the cut-out shape.

3 Next, drill a hole through the side of each hand, as shown in fig. 1, with a $3/32$in drill. You must take great care to drill centrally. If you are using a hand drill, it would be easier for someone to hold the rope climber steady for you while you drill as otherwise, you are likely to go off-centre. If you are using a vice (vise) for this operation, remember to cover the jaws of the vice (vise), so as not to make fancy patterns on your workpiece. If, on the other hand, you are using an electric drill, there should be no problems, but do take your time. Just gently drill your holes a little at a time, all the way through the wood. Make sure that your holes are clean because later on you have to thread your string through these.

4 Paint both sides of your rope climber and, when dry, varnish him.

(instructions are continued on page 38)

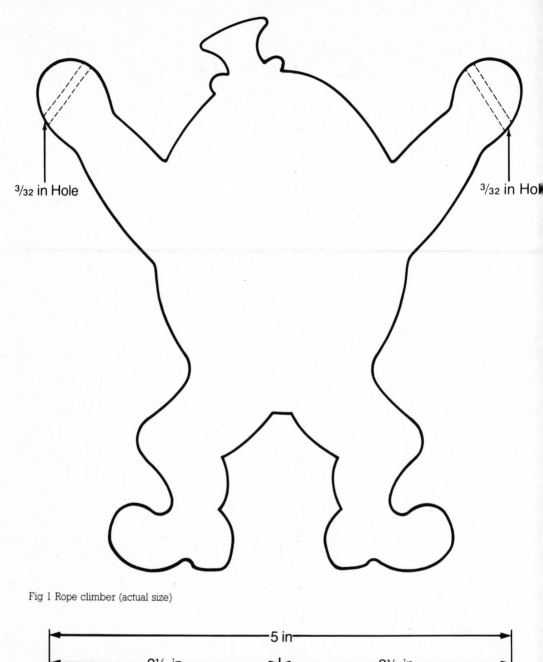

³/₃₂ in Hole

³/₃₂ in Hol

Fig 1 Rope climber (actual size)

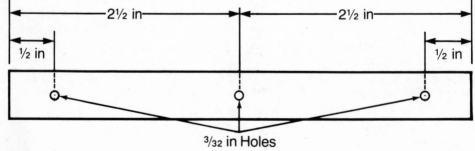

Fig 2 Bar

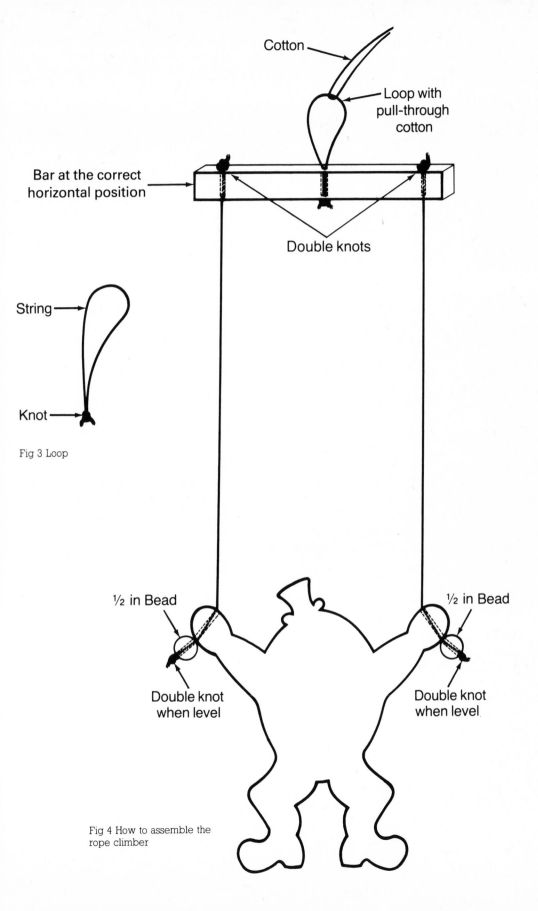

Cotton

Loop with pull-through cotton

Bar at the correct horizontal position

Double knots

String

Knot

Fig 3 Loop

½ in Bead

½ in Bead

Double knot when level

Double knot when level

Fig 4 How to assemble the rope climber

5 Now for your length of ramin bar, which helps to hold your rope climber aloft, and aids him to climb. Using the drawing shown in fig. 2, measure and mark out. Drill the holes, using a ³⁄₃₂in drill, and again ensure that your holes are clean. Now glasspaper and varnish this.

6 Assembly time again (as shown in fig. 4)! Firstly, take your 6in piece of braided cord, fold it in half and knot the two loose ends together securely (see fig. 3). This will become your hook with which to hang your rope climber. Having done that, thread your cord through the centre hole of your bar. To do this, take a strong thin piece of cotton and loop it through the loop of the cord. Don't knot it. Take the two loose ends of cotton and thread them through the centre hole of the bar. Then pull your looped cord through and pull tight to ensure that your knot will not come undone. Next, take one of your 36in pieces of braided cord and thread through one hand of the rope climber and then through one side of the bar, and double knot. Put one of your beads on the other end of your cord, and tie a loose knot only at this stage. (This will prevent the cord coming out of the hand.) Then do exactly the same with the other cord.

7 Before you secure all your knots, ensure that your rope climber is hanging absolutely level (nothing looks worse than a drunken-looking Humpty Dumpty). Hang Humpty on the wall, and if he is level the bar will be at the horizontal position as shown in fig. 4. Now, if the bar hangs low on one side, all you have to do is to lower the knot with the bead, until this becomes level. When you

have achieved this, double knot below the beads and, lastly, glue all your knots.

Important When you come to hang Humpty Dumpty in his final position, always make sure that the body of the rope climber is roughly the same height as the children's faces. This is because (although a faint possibility, nonetheless we would like to leave nothing to chance where children's safety is concerned) it just might be possible that a child could get his head jammed between the cord if the position of the rope climber is too low on the wall.

Now, to make him climb, just hold the beads at the bottom, in each hand, keeping both cords taut. Then pull down on one side, and then the other side, and he begins to climb upwards. This is just like milking a goat. We speak with some authority on the matter as we were once at an agricultural show demonstrating the rope climber, and said that its climbing is just like milking a cow. 'Indeed it isn't', said a lady, who turned out to be a farmer's wife and an expert on the subject of milking both goats and cows. She showed us the difference by milking a goat and a cow for us later. She was absolutely right – a goat it is! Happy climbing, folks!

Materials
1 piece ¼in plywood, 6in×5½in
1 length ramin, ½in× ½in×5in
2 pieces braided cord, each 36in long
1 piece braided cord 6in long
two ½in wooden beads

---

6 Jumping Jacks
Colour plate 3

This is one of the most ancient toys known to mankind. It is frankly impossible even to guess at its origin. We know that many cultures throughout the world used it one time or another in different ways.

The toy's workings depend upon the simple, but immensely effective, bodily movements that are produced when the cord is pulled, jerked and released. The best known example of the jumping jack is the Russian Bear, which has been popular for centuries. Also well known is the human, or animal, mask with an articulated jaw. When the string is pulled (and with the aid of a swift bit of ventriloquism) the result can be extremely effective. This type of jumping jack was probably used by quick-witted priests in ancient times, when credulous people came to consult the oracle. In a darkened cave or room, lit only by flickering torchlight, with a touch of mist introduced to blur and obscure clear outlines and a little incense wafting around, combined with a hollow tube to produce a metallic 'spirit voice', the results must have been stunning – and the jumping jack would have really come into his own. Fake mediums used this idea to great effect in some of the notorious fake seances in the nineteenth century (which only goes to prove that there is still one born every minute!).

We were so impressed by the idea of the articulated jaw, that we created one of our own – Fred Phanakapan. We tried it out on an unsuspecting public at a large craft show, where we hung one prominently in view. Anthony, who has a beard and moustache, and whose lips are therefore seldom seen, gave Fred a good build-up, culminating in a deeply moving rendering of that old cockney favourite, 'Your baby has fell down the plughole'. This emerged as something like, 'Oar paybee azvel dawn the blugole', and they all wanted to have a go at it as well. We sold the toys very quickly that day.

There is also the 'Hanged Man', at least three hundred years old. This is a cut-out shape of a man pinned to the outline of a gallows, noosed. When the string is pulled, the figure dances in the most macabre way – not at all suitable for children, except, perhaps, the one or two that we know! The fourth well-known figure, and perhaps the most spectacular of all is the 'Dancing Skeleton', known as Bones. These toys make marvellous effective shadow puppets when suspended from a cord in a dim room and lit by a spotlight, or accompanied by a flickering candle. When the cord is tugged in rhythm, the doll dances startlingly well. Handicapped children derive great satisfaction from this toy because of the extreme simplicity in its mode of operation.

In eighteenth-century France, the jumping jack (then known as a *pantin* or *pantine*) became quite the rage – the 'in thing' to own. Voluminous-skirted dancing ladies, pirates, highwaymen, bewigged nobles and a various assortment of exotic animals and birds were some of the most popular types. The French government of the day considered banning this toy at one time because of its alleged propensity to cause pregnant ladies to miscarry. In the nineteenth century, paper cut-outs of the jacks were printed in bulk, on cardboard sheets, and sold in the vast toyshops and emporiums of Victorian England; price, one penny plain, or twopence coloured.

String marionettes probably evolved from jumping jacks. It takes only a little imagination to envisage carved, shaped and painted figures, now three-dimensional, with their jointed and articulated parts having attached strings to control each individual limb. The Germans called the jacks '*Hampelmann*'; and to 'play the *Hampelmann*' was 'to string someone along', or 'to pull strings to achieve your own ends'.

The ideas for creating simple jumping jacks are endless. Here are a few for you to try later: bird; bear; ballerina; crocodile; and, for adults, two of our most popular jacks are a well-endowed lady of the naughty nineties – our 'Southern Belle' – and a muscular circus 'Strong Man'. Whatever you choose, have fun!

For now, we have three types for you to make: Humpty Dumpty; the clown; and, would you believe it, the bowler hat that winks!

Humpty Dumpty

Humpty Dumpty sat on a wall.
Humpty Dumpty had a great fall.
All the king's horses and all the king's men
Couldn't put Humpty together again.

(Traditional)

We have yet to find a child who does not like Humpty Dumpty, or, as our Richard always calls him, 'Humpety Dumpety'.

The Clown
Anthony designed the clown. He took his inspiration from seeing a truly marvellous sculpture of a clown in a craft exhibition some years ago. The craftsman in question had captured the Chaplinesque qualities of the truly great clown. The down-at-heel, but ever hopeful aspects of everyday life. And the banana-skin game: 'if it happens to me – it's a tragedy – if it happens to you – hilarity.'

And so Anthony returned home and designed this superb laughter-maker, whose string is just itching to be pulled, to make him happily dance around.

The bowler hat that winks
The bowler hat that winks is one of our speciality jumping jacks. It came about when we were down at the fleamarket one day, browsing. On one of the stalls I caught sight of a battered old bowler hat perched rakishly on the stallholder's head. This fascinated me. I have always had secret ambitions to be a song-and-dance man, and the hat could have made my act complete. Apart from the facts that (a) I am the wrong sex, and (b) can neither sing nor dance well, they do not deter me from trying – and I can be very trying. Anthony, to my disgust, refused to enter into negotiations with the aforementioned stallholder for the sale of his bowler. He was deaf to all my entreaties, and, as I had no money of my own, I arrived home hatless. Still sulking from my defeat there, our friend George came to visit us that evening. He possesses the instant ability to cheer me up; he winks at me often (he winks at everyone else also). Suddenly, I achieved instant inspiration, and rushed to my drawing board. There emerged, very shortly afterwards, this design for the unique 'Bowler Hat that Winks'!

(*instructions begin on page 44*)

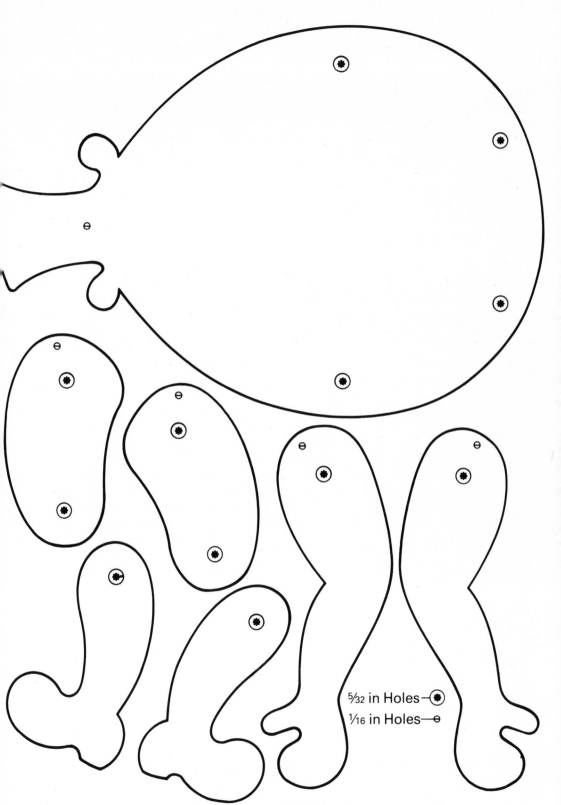

5/32 in Holes —⊛
1/16 in Holes —⊖

Fig 1A Humpty Dumpty jumping jack (actual size)

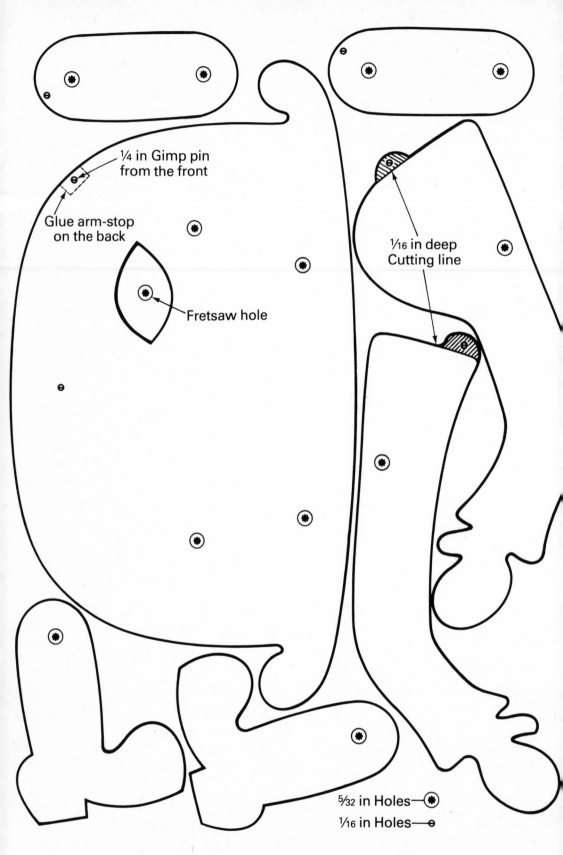

Fig 1B The bowler hat that winks jumping jack (actual size)

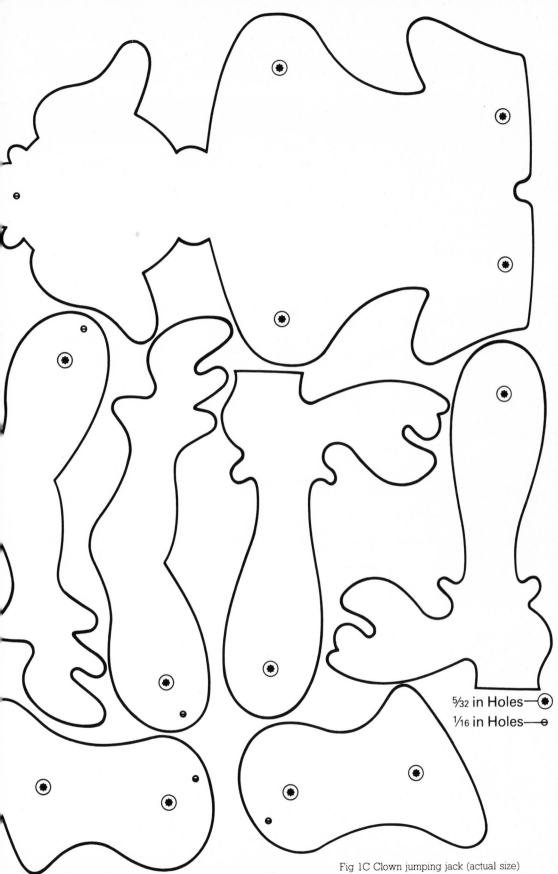

5/32 in Holes—⊛
1/16 in Holes—⊖

Fig 1C Clown jumping jack (actual size)

Method

We have illustrated three of our most popular jumping jacks: Humpty Dumpty; the bowler hat that winks; and the clown (shown in figs. 1A, 1B and 1C). In order not to cause any confusion, the basic instructions for the making of the clown and Humpty Dumpty are the same. For the making of the bowler hat, there will be just two extra instructions: the making and fitting of the arm-stop, and the all-important marking out of the eyes. These will be pointed out to you in instruction nos 5 and 6. Fear not, they are all very simple to make. All you have to do now is to choose which jumping jack you intend to create. If you are feeling ambitious, then you can make all three together.

1 Cut your tracing paper to the same size as your ⅛in plywood, that is to say 7in× 10in. This will make handling easier. Now trace out your choice of jumping jack from one of the figs. 1A, 1B or 1C, not forgetting also to mark out all the holes shown in the diagram. (For the bowler hat, mark the position of the arm-stop.) You should now have seven pieces traced out and, if not, double check!

Next, pencil the reverse side of your tracing paper, and then place this squarely on to your ⅛in piece of plywood. Tape the four corners to your plywood, and this will prevent the paper from moving. Then continue to transfer the outline from paper to wood.

2 Before you commence cutting out the wood, drill all your holes marked out as illustrated in figs. 1A, 1B and 1C. You require ⅟₁₆in holes for your string, and ⁵⁄₃₂in holes for your rivets. (If you are making the bowler hat, then you will also need a ⁵⁄₃₂in hole in the centre of the right eye in the bowler hat – see fig. 1B. This will allow your fretsaw blade to enter, and enable you to cut out the eye-piece later.)

3 Now you can take your hand fretsaw, and cut out all your seven sections. (If you are making the bowler hat, do not forget to cut out your eye-piece. To do this, release only the top wing nut of your fretsaw, and release the blade. Then push the loose end of the blade through the eye holes, as shown in fig.

1B. Now refit your blade, and proceed to cut out your eye shape. When you have finished cutting, release one end of the blade, and remove from the workpiece. Now refit the blade to the fretsaw in readiness for the next step.)

4 We have now to remove a small section from the arms and legs (and this will be quite painless.) To do this, take the arms and the top half of the legs (thigh to knees) and lay them out (as shown in fig. 2). Mark a line on each arm and leg, ³⁄₁₆in from the top. Take your craft knife and cut along your line, just ⅟₁₆in deep. (This is approximately the thickness of the top ply.) Then, using your wood chisel, remove the shaded area shown in fig. 2. (For the bowler-hat arms, shown in

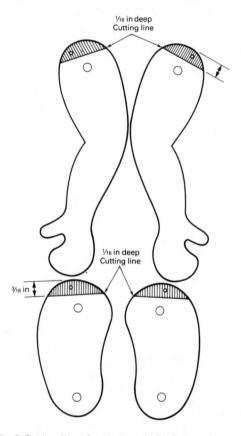

Fig 2 Cutting lines for jumping jacks' legs and arms; bowler hat arms shown in Fig 1B

Fig 3 Cut a recess on the bowler hat arms

fig. 1B, you will then have a recess, or step, as shown in fig 3. This allows enough clearance for your string, and will not impede the movements of the arms and legs.) Now you can give your jumping jack a good sandpapering, and remove all the accrued wood dust.

5 **For those who are making the bowler hat only.** To prevent the arm moving over too far, which would result in a failure to obtain a successful wink (and we wouldn't want this to happen), just fit a small stop (as shown in fig. 1B). To do this, you will need a piece of ⅛in plywood, gleaned from your wood scrap. This will measure ⅜in×³⁄₁₆in. Trim your ½in gimp pin down to ¼in, using the side cutters on your pliers. Put a little wood glue on the body, and place the ⅛in×⅜in×³⁄₁₆in arm stop at the position marked in fig. 1B. Then, from the front side, knock in your gimp pin, to make the stop completely secure.

6 **Bowler hat only.** To mark out your winking eye, take one of your ⅛in rivets, and push this in through the hole in the hat (shown in fig. 4). Push on to this your eye arm, and let your arm drop downwards, until it reaches the stop (see fig. 4). Now for an artistic bit. Using your pencil, lightly draw the outline of the eye surround. Push the arm upwards (as shown in fig. 5), until the arm reaches the stop. Then lightly draw in your second eye surround. Remove the arm now, and the eyes should resemble those in fig. 6.

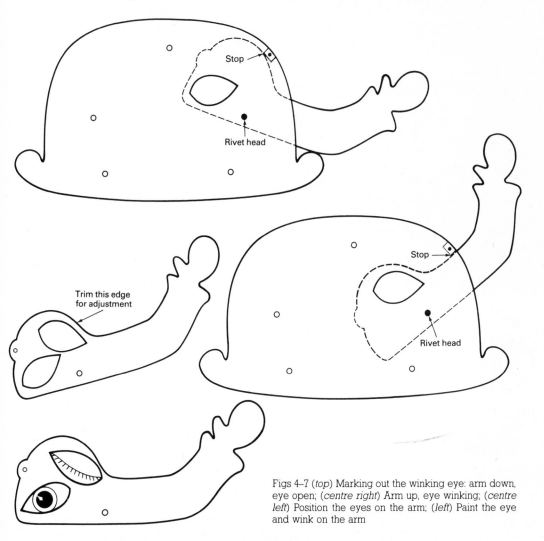

Figs 4–7 (*top*) Marking out the winking eye: arm down, eye open; (*centre right*) Arm up, eye winking; (*centre left*) Position the eyes on the arm; (*left*) Paint the eye and wink on the arm

If your eye surrounds overlap, not to worry. All you have to do is to trim a little wood from the edge of the arm (as shown in fig. 6.) Then you can go ahead, and re-mark the eyes.

7 Now paint your jumping jack as brightly as possible, preferably adding contrasting colours and patterns, as the movements, when in action, will be far more dramatic and pronounced. (If you are painting the bowler hat, remember that the wink is at the top of the arm-piece, and the open eye is at the base, see eye-and-wink sketch – fig. 7. Do remember to paint both eyes the same colour, otherwise the results can look distinctly odd! Then varnish.)

8 Assembly instructions for all jumping jacks. These are particularly easy to do, so don't panic. First, clean out all the rivet holes of any paint or varnish that may be stuck there, using either a small round file or a 5/32in drill. Also, clean out your 1/16in string holes at the same time. You will need a hard block to hammer over the edges of the rivets. The simplest way to do this is to use a large hammer head as the block, and a small hammer to round off your rivets (see fig. 8). Take the top and lower legs, remembering that the upper leg is placed on top of the lower leg (as shown in fig. 8, front and side plan); rest the head of the rivet on your large hammer head and, using your smaller hammer, gently tap around the edge of the rivet to form a mushroom shape. (Make sure that the legs you have riveted together are not too tight, but move around freely and easily.) When you have done this, repeat the action with the second leg. Now, take one piece of your 6in long string and tie a double knot at one end. Having done this, thread the other end of the string through the 1/16in hole in one of the legs, starting at point A, fig. 9. Then thread through the other 1/16in hole in the second leg; finishing with your tying a loose knot at point B. Then continue to do the same with the arms. You may now rivet the assembled legs to the body, and also the arms.

To adjust the arms and legs of your jumping jack so that they hang correctly, just lay him face down and place the arms and legs, in the positions shown in fig. 10. Push the loose knot tightly down to the string holes on your legs and arms, and tie a double knot.

Now for your pull string that will control all the movements of your jumping jack. Take your 10in piece of string, and knot one end securely to the centre of the arm string (point A, fig. 10). Pass the pull string underneath the leg string, and secure this to the centre of the leg string (point B). And now, hold your jumping jack aloft and pull at the string. If you have followed the instructions, the arms and legs should move together easily. Everything works? Yes; jolly good. Slight difficulty? If the arms rise up easily, but you have little leg movement, just adjust this by releasing the knot slightly on the leg string (point B), and move the position of the knot slightly downwards along the pull string to give more slack between the horizontal string position (point C), and this will correct the fault. If, on the other hand, the legs rise up with little arm movements, then all you need to do is to reverse the procedure. Release the knot at the centre of the leg string (point B) and, by moving the knot slightly up the pull string, this in turn will take up the slack at point C.

When you have achieved equal movement of the arms and legs, you can then thread the remaining string through the hole in the hat, and double knot this to form a loop. All you have to do now is to fit your wooden bead at the end of your pull string and tie securely. Finally, glue all your knots to secure. Hang up your jumping jack, and away you go, all ready for play!

Materials

1 piece 1/8in plywood, 7in × 10in
1 piece 1/8in plywood, 3/8in × 3/16in
one 1/2in gimp pin
6 flat headed rivets, 1/8in diameter × 7/16in long
3 pieces strong string, 1/16in × 6in long
1 piece strong string, 1/16in × 10in long
one 3/8in wooden bead

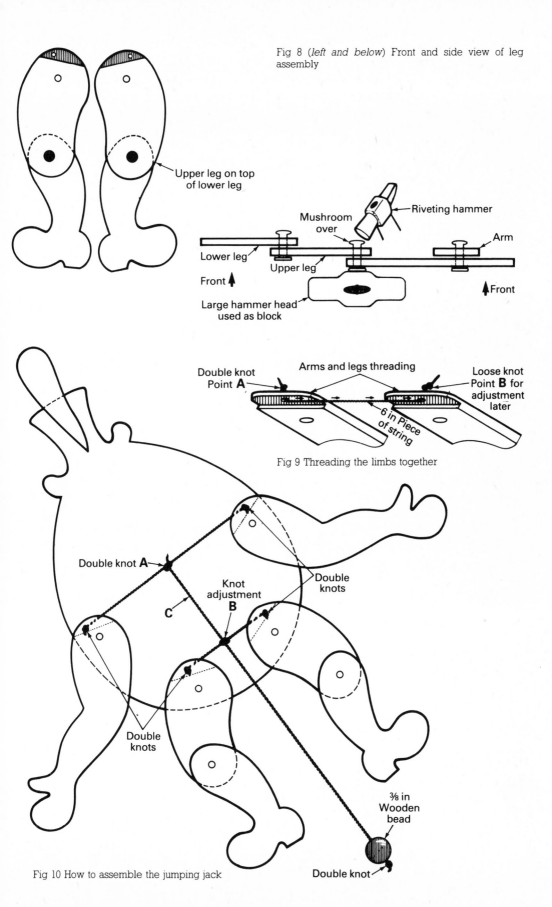

Fig 8 (*left and below*) Front and side view of leg assembly

Upper leg on top of lower leg

Riveting hammer

Mushroom over

Arm

Lower leg

Upper leg

Front

Front

Large hammer head used as block

Double knot Point **A**

Arms and legs threading

Loose knot Point **B** for adjustment later

6 in Piece of string

Fig 9 Threading the limbs together

Double knot **A**

Knot adjustment **B**

Double knots

C

Double knots

⅜ in Wooden bead

Double knot

Fig 10 How to assemble the jumping jack

7 The Polly Parrot Tumbler
Colour plate 2

We had been making balancing parrots for some time when, one day, Anthony had a bright idea: what happens, he thought, holding the cut-out parrot shape in front of him, if I insert a wooden dowel through its body, tie string to each end of the dowel, hang it up, and twirl the figure to the top of the string? What happened was that we experimented and, having found the centre of gravity (so that the toy worked properly) we made our very first polly parrot tumbler. We thought we had invented a new toy, but one day at a show we met an elderly gentleman who told us that he remembered this type of toy being sold in his childhood, back in the early thirties. The ones he had seen depicted clown tumblers; they were considerably larger and heavier than ours, and were made to work by tapping the clown's feet smartly with a stick.

We created these toys originally as superior mobiles for babies; even a little child can reach up and make them work. Then we found that adults love them too, as they can be hung up anywhere in the house. They are also a great favourite with handicapped people of all ages.

The parrot can be set in motion in two ways. He can be tapped smartly on the head or tail to make him tumble, or the ball at the end of the dowel can be twisted upwards in a rapid motion, causing him to tumble up and down, around and around, again and again. The parrot will keep moving for a whole minute – we've timed it!

When you have made your parrot, paint him as brightly as possible. The more colours used, the more he will resemble a coloured rainbow when in motion. There are many different creatures which can be used to make this tumbling toy – dogs, cats, clowns or rabbits – provided that the centre of gravity is inserted in the appropriate place in each one. And now – without further ado – follow the instructions and make your very own polly parrot tumbler.

Method

1 Draw around the shape of the parrot on tracing paper, and then transfer the shape onto the plywood, as shown in fig. 1A.

2 Drill a $3/16$in hole in the plywood, in the exact spot shown in fig. 1B. This is the centre of gravity; if the hole is drilled anywhere else, the toy will not work.

3 Cut the parrot shape out using a hand fretsaw. Take your time; the cutting must be accurate to achieve a good balance.

4 When you have done this, glasspaper the parrot shape until it is completely smooth; your parrot is now ready for painting. Make him as bright as possible in many colours, and varnish him on each side for that extra shine.

5 Now for the perch. Cut the dowelling to the exact length shown in fig. 2. It is a good idea to trim the edges of the dowelling slightly with a pencil sharpener at this stage; it will make it easier to fit the beads at each end later.

6 Measure $1/2$in from each end of the dowel, and drill a $3/16$in hole at each end for the cords (see fig. 2A).

7 Drill a $3/16$in hole through each of the two beads (fig. 2B).

8 Thread one end of the cord through the hole in the dowelling, and tie a double knot to secure. Put a little wood glue in the first bead, and push it firmly onto the end of the dowel.

9 Push the bar through the hole drilled in the parrot, making sure that it is a good snug fit. Position the parrot just before the centre line (fig. 2c).

10 Thread the other end of the cord through the dowel, and double knot as before. Glue the second bead to this end of the dowel. Hold the cord at the top, check that everything is level, and make a loop at the top of the cord. Finally, put a little wood glue around the centre point of the bar, and push the parrot right onto the centre line. If you need to adjust the parrot at this stage, hold the parrot and slightly twist the bar backwards and forwards until properly balanced. The parrot can either be upright or leaning slightly forwards. Allow the glue to dry thoroughly and the parrot is ready.

Materials
1 piece ⅛in plywood, 6in × 4in
1 piece dowelling, 4½in × ³⁄₁₆in
two ½in wooden beads
1 piece strong cord, 36in long × ¹⁄₁₆in thick

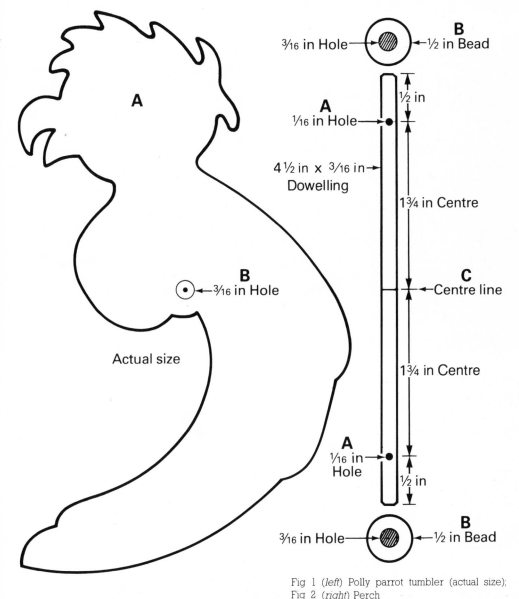

Fig 1 (*left*) Polly parrot tumbler (actual size);
Fig 2 (*right*) Perch

8 The Balancing Parrot
Colour plate 2

This toy has been giving joy for many hundreds of years. The older versions that we have seen usually depict rearing stallions or unicorns. These were made to balance on the very edge of a table, or shelf. Each had a long wire attached to the body, curving downwards, which was attached to a fixed, weighted pendulum – usually a lump of lead. Other balancing toys of yore included monkeys, cockatoos and even crocodiles – in fact any creature with a long tail lends itself admirably to this concept. These toys enjoyed great popularity among the Victorians; parrots were fashioned in enormous sizes on gigantic perches – large enough incidentally to concuss any small child easily!

People put these toys now to varied uses. One elderly lady told us that she was buying a balancing parrot to keep her cockatoo company. She happily walked off with her purchase, leaving us with so many unanswered questions that our minds began to boggle. Why didn't she just go out and buy another cockatoo, we wondered. Are cockatoos awfully expensive? And, what would happen when she placed our parrot in the cockatoo's cage. Would the cockatoo go dizzy watching the balancing parrot swing backwards and forwards? And how would he or she feel, when he found that the parrot wouldn't speak to him, or her? Someone else bought one for their friend, a retired sea captain. Straightaway, we imagined her buying it for someone like Captain Cat, from Dylan Thomas's *Under Milk Wood*, with him saying something like, 'here is a pretty polly parrot, very nice, that I can put on top of my shoulder, or hold on my seaman's finger, and it will keep me company, and nicely snug all through the blackest dark, moonless black shaded winter's nights, that ever came by.' Eat your heart out, Rosie Probert!

We had a terrible job, at first, making these, until we cracked the problem of creating the point of balance. Having done this, they will then balance so nicely that you can hold them on the very tip of your finger and set them moving, and they will not fall off. What is the best way to sell them, we pondered. Anthony evolved a sure and certain method, after I had read and had become deeply affected by the book *Treasure Island*. First, he stood with a bird balanced on one of his fingers, then pretended to feed it birdseed, and all the while, talked to it. This aroused a certain amount of interest from the general public for a start. Then he squeaked 'pretty Polly!', from the corner of his mouth. People who remembered the balancing birds from the days of their youth, and, indeed, anyone who had never seen a performance such as this one before, were equally delighted, especially when Anthony suddenly launched into his Robert Newton act. Robert Newton, for anyone who does not know of him, was a superb actor, and the only definitive Long John Silver on film. Anyway, accelerating into 'pieces of eight', and 'fifteen men on the dead man's chest', and also 'Yo ho ho, and a bottle of rum' and, what with whipping up excitement to fever pitch by addressing anyone and everyone as 'Jim Lad', the long and the short of it is that we managed to sell the entire stock of balancing parrots that very day!

There are many more complex variations to the balancing-parrot toys that we have made. The best of them is a parrot that rolls his eyes, sways his cockscomb, and even gnashes his beak as well, with a penetratingly but hypnotic 'clicking' sound. But, just for now, back to simplicity.

Before you attempt to make any single figure that appeals to you from wood, say sea-horse, acrobat or moon, do be warned. Try out your initial idea on card, or hardboard first, to make sure that your figure balances correctly. For, it *must* balance absolutely accurately in order to work properly, and to swing to and fro. This simple tip will, we assure you, save you endless hours of otherwise muttered curses of frustration!

Method

Before you start making your balancing parrot, we would like to give you a little piece of advice. We have illustrated the correct way in which to balance the parrot on his perch, and also the incorrect way, because some people may be tempted to take a short cut. Just cut out the parrot, leaving a nice pointed end on your plywood, as shown in fig. 1A. If the parrot is made in this way, you will be dreadfully disappointed, because what will happen is this. The point will chip away in next to no time, and the parrot will wobble from side to side, and then fall from his perch – a few choice words will then be said by your family about your skills as a toymaker! So, build the bird the correct way, as shown, in fig. 1B.

Fig 1 Make sure you balance the parrot correctly on his perch

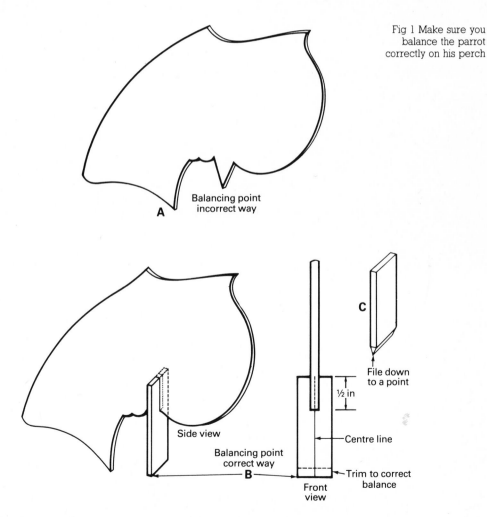

Balancing point
incorrect way

A

C

File down
to a point

Side view

Balancing point
correct way

Centre line

½ in

Trim to correct
balance

B

Front
view

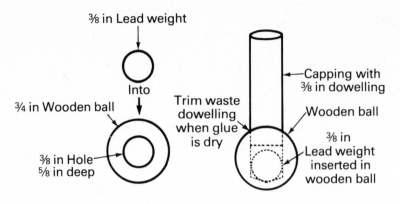

Fig 2 Assembling the weight

1 Before you do any marking out, or cutting out, take your ¾in wooden ball and drill a ⅜in hole centrally in it, to a depth of ⅝in, as shown in fig. 2A. To achieve the correct depth, all you have to do is measure upwards from the tip of your drill ⅝in, then wind tape around the drill bit at this point, and this will act as your depth gauge. After drilling your hole, place into it your ⅜in lead weight, as shown in fig. 2B. Cap this by using a piece of your ⅜in dowelling. Put a little wood glue around the hole in your wooden ball, and push in the dowelling. Put this to one side, and leave it to dry thoroughly and completely before trimming off any excess dowelling.

2 Take your tracing paper, and cut off a piece 8½in×4in, then place this on the pattern of your parrot, see fig. 3, and carefully trace out, not forgetting to mark the all-important position of the cut-out centre line, as shown in fig. 3A. Having traced out your parrot shape and pencilled the reverse side of the tracing paper to give a clearer image, place the pattern squarely on to your ⅛in plywood, and secure by taping the edges to your piece of wood. Then transfer the outline of the parrot to your plywood.

3 Before beginning to cut out your parrot, first take your piece of hardwood, 1½in× ½in× 1⁄16in thickness (or your lollipop stick, cut to size). *Important note*: before cutting this, remember to cut down the grain of wood, and not across, otherwise you will weaken the strength of the wood con-

siderably. Place this edge down, as shown in fig. 4, along the cut-out centre line that you have marked (shown in fig. 3A). Using a sharp pencil, mark out the correct thickness of the balance support piece on to your parrot, as shown in fig. 4. Take your hand fretsaw, and carefully cut out your parrot shape. When you come to your cut-out slot, you must cut to the *inside* of the lines. This will give you a snug fit for your balancing support. Now that you have done this, and cut out the shape, don't forget to smooth the edges. Apart from offering less wind resistance when toing and froing, nothing looks worse than to see a painted toy full of wood burrs at the edges.

4 You can now fit your 1½in× ½in× 1⁄16in thick piece of hardwood, or lollipop stick, which is your balancing parrot's support piece. First, make a centre line as shown in fig. 3B. Next, put a little wood glue into the cut-out slot on your parrot, as shown in fig. 3A. Take your parrot support piece and push this into the cut-out slot, and keep it completely central, as shown in fig. 1B.

5 Take your wooden ball, making sure that the glue is well and truly dry, and cut off your waste dowelling. Then glasspaper the capping level on the wooden ball. Cut a slot ⅛in wide and 3⁄16in deep, using your hand fretsaw, as shown in fig. 3c.

6 This paragraph deals with actually balancing the parrot. Just place the wooden ball on to the tail of the parrot, at approximately the point shown in fig. 3D. And now

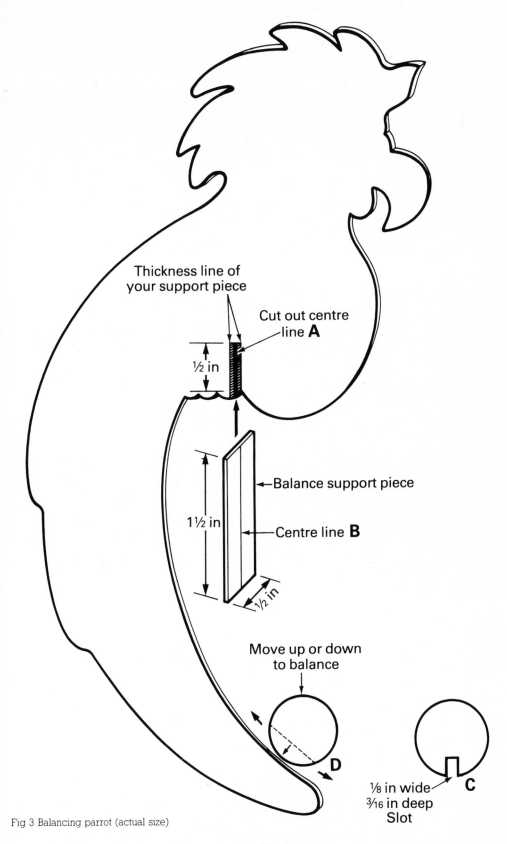

Thickness line of
your support piece

Cut out centre
line **A**

½ in

Balance support piece

1½ in

Centre line **B**

½ in

Move up or down
to balance

D

⅛ in wide
³⁄₁₆ in deep
Slot

C

Fig 3 Balancing parrot (actual size)

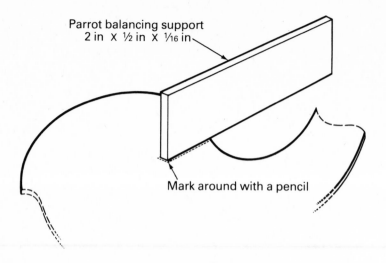

Parrot balancing support
2 in X ½ in X ⅟₁₆ in

Mark around with a pencil

Fig 4 Marking out cut-out lines

for the moment of truth. Balance the parrot on your index finger, and set him swinging gently. If he rocks back and forth perfectly, then you have no problems. If, however, the bird falls backwards or forwards, just correct this deficiency in balance by moving the ball either just further up the tail, or further down the tail, and you should now have a parrot that balances and swings well. You still haven't? Not to worry. All that you have to do is to trim a small section from the end of the balance support piece – see fig. 1B. Then repeat this procedure with the wooden ball, until he balances well. Now you can glue your wooden ball on to the tail. Then file the end of your balance support piece to a point. This is shown in fig. 1C.

7 And now the painting of the parrot. Remember that bold colours and a couple of thick dark lines, bright highlights and contrasts are the order of the day here. You don't have to be an expert to paint Polly, just go ahead and do something rainbowy and fiery-bright. Then varnish the bird.

8 Now that you have completed the parrot successfully, we shall concentrate upon his perch. All three sections of the perch are shown in fig. 5, complete with measurements, so there should be no difficulties. Just start with your hardwood block, fig. 5A, and mark out as shown. Then drill your ½in hole ¾in deep, using the guide method as

described in instruction no. 1. When you have done this, chamfer the edges, then glasspaper, and put to one side. Take your ½in dowelling as in fig. 5B, and mark out as shown. Drill your ⁵⁄₁₆in hole ⁷⁄₁₆in deep. Glasspaper this, not forgetting to take off the edges of the end pieces. Place this to one side, together with your block.

Now for the last piece of dowelling shown in fig. 5C. Once again, mark out as shown. Then use your hand fretsaw, and cut out the shaded area shown in fig. 5C, to a depth of approximately ³⁄₁₆in. This will then become the platform on which your parrot will stand swaying. Use your pencil sharpener to take the rough edges away from your ⁵⁄₁₆in dowelling. Glasspaper this piece.

9 Assembly time again – as shown in fig. 6. First, put a little wood glue around the holes in your hardwood block and in the ½in dowelling. Then fit the ⁵⁄₁₆in dowelling into the hole in the ½in dowelling, and the ½in dowelling into the hole in the block – all shown in figs. 6A and 6B. Make sure that all the pieces are squarely inserted and that the platform perch is entirely level. We don't want the parrot sliding down his stand. When all is dry, varnish the whole perch.

Having already painted and varnished your parrot, and having assembled his perch, there is only one thing left to do now, and that is to put the two together – parrot

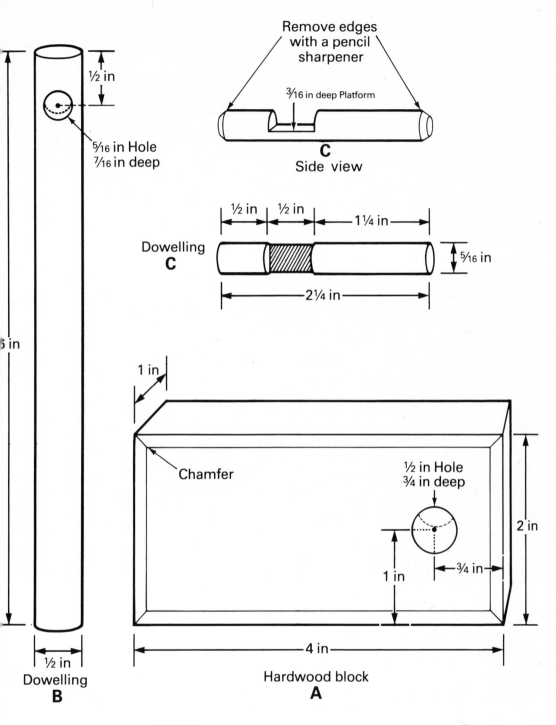

½ in

⁵⁄₁₆ in Hole
⁷⁄₁₆ in deep

Remove edges
with a pencil
sharpener

³⁄₁₆ in deep Platform

C
Side view

½ in ½ in 1¼ in

Dowelling
C

⁵⁄₁₆ in

2¼ in

1 in

Chamfer

½ in Hole
¾ in deep

2 in

1 in ¾ in

4 in

Hardwood block
A

6 in

½ in
Dowelling
B

Fig 5 Stand for balancing parrot (actual size)

onto perch. If Polly still won't balance, this can only be due to the added weight of the paint and varnish. So just remove a little fraction more from the end of your balance support piece.

You can also place your parrot on the very edge of a shelf. Or, make more than one parrot and place them on the branches of a Christmas tree, or sturdy house plant, to give a jungly effect. The sky is the limit now that you have made your first balancing parrot.

Materials
one ¾in wooden ball
one ⅜in lead weight
1 short piece ⅜in dowelling
1 piece ⅛in plywood 8½in×4in
1 piece hardwood 1½in×½in×approx ¹⁄₁₆in thick (or 1 lollipop stick cut to size)

Perch
1 piece hardwood 4in×2in×1in
1 length dowelling 6in×½in
1 length dowelling 2¼in×⁵⁄₁₆in

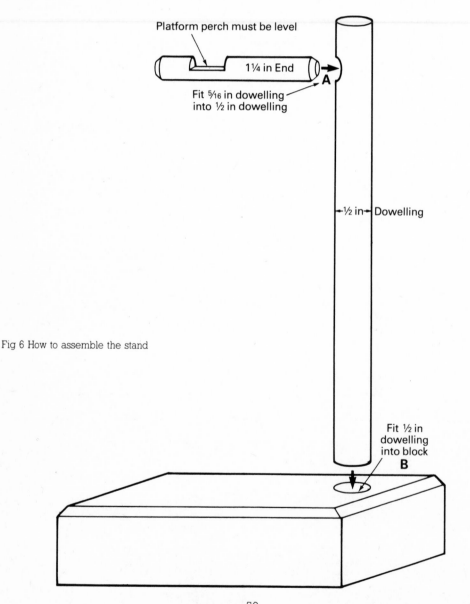

Platform perch must be level

1¼ in End

A

Fit ⁵⁄₁₆ in dowelling into ½ in dowelling

½ in Dowelling

Fig 6 How to assemble the stand

Fit ½ in dowelling into block

B

9 Acrobat on Sticks, Stand and Bars

Colour plate 4

This moving folk toy is a classic of its kind, an all-time favourite, and just as popular with adults as with children. The origin of this toy probably dates back to ancient Greece, where it was known, not unsurprisingly enough perhaps, as the Greek acrobat. Variations of this same theme that we have seen, encompass two figures suspended from strings, facing each other, and appearing to wrestle when they are set in motion. In the nineteenth century, caricatures of the two leading British political opponents of the day were in vogue – those of William Gladstone and Benjamin Disraeli.

Instead of having human figures, the tops of the sticks can be made into the shape of palm fronds, with the interior containing two radiantly glowing parrots. This is known as the South American variation. There is also a carved and jointed acrobat, an early German version, facing forwards, whose arms dangle down from a bar and who is supported by sticks inserted into a solid wooden base. The doll is propelled up and over the bar, by means of winding up a handle inset into the bar.

As well as being a superb plaything, the acrobat has many other practical uses. He is extremely popular with adults suffering from mental stress. We understand from many of our customers that this toy induces a state of relaxation. It works as a marvellous therapeutic device for stroke victims, to exercise their wasted hand muscles, and also for handicapped people.

The normal way to use the toy is to squeeze and release the base of the sticks, and the acrobat performs many exciting physical movements. Now, as you will see,

we have included four types of acrobat in this chapter: two acrobats on sticks; one acrobat on stand; and one on bars. These should cover everyone's needs – for the very young, for handicapped children and adults. Choose the one that will best suit you. The first one is the simple acrobat on sticks, which we call the H type. Secondly, we have a recent version, called the Japanese acrobat. This one is based on an early twentieth-century Japanese rabbit folk toy, and utilises cane for the sticks. The third acrobat is the acrobat on stand, which we have designed to enable you to fit a spring, which will assist those who may be handicapped in any way and may find difficulty in

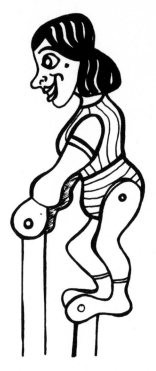

squeezing the sticks. This is a much sturdier version of the toy. Fourthly, the acrobat on bars, which is sturdier and was evolved from an early German version, which we mentioned earlier. The original version of this had a handle with which to propel the doll figure up and over the bars. We have done away with this concept of the handle, and used beads in its stead.

The measurements of the acrobats on sticks, stand and bars are average. However, before making any toy for a special child or handicapped person, make sure that the width of both sticks will fit the individual's size of hand. In other words, tailor-make this toy to suit individual size and need. A normal child can, however, easily use this toy as soon as he reaches two and a half to three years of age, and some chil-

dren, we have found, can easily cope with it from the age of two.

Other versions that you may like to make later involve a monkey figure, and a giant whizzer shape on strings, which fits inside the sticks. Now, all that you have to do is to choose which acrobat you wish to make, then go on to choose the stand, sticks or bars from which he will begin his varied assortment of acrobatic tricks and gymnastics that will dazzle and amaze you! Make your acrobat figure first, as we show you. He is adaptable to whatever sticks or stand that you choose to use. Then we show you how to make each stick or stand. (The assembly and completion of the acrobat on bars is dealt with in its own section.) Finally, we demonstrate how to knit the two together; acrobat to sticks or stand, in the last section.

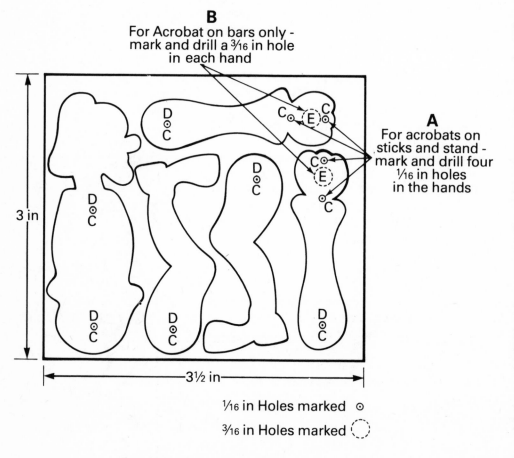

B
For Acrobat on bars only -
mark and drill a ³⁄₁₆ in hole
in each hand

A
For acrobats on sticks and stand -
mark and drill four ¹⁄₁₆ in holes
in the hands

3 in

3½ in

¹⁄₁₆ in Holes marked ⊙

³⁄₁₆ in Holes marked ⟨ ⟩

Fig 1 Acrobat figure (actual size) for sticks, stand and bar

ACROBAT
Method

Take your tracing paper. At this point, do not cut a piece exactly the same size as your plywood. The reason is, as the acrobat covers such a relatively small area upon which you will be tracing, you will need that extra paper to hold and keep steady while tracing out the pattern. To continue, place your tracing paper on to the acrobat and carefully trace out the five sections, plus the surround line, as shown in fig. 1. Also, mark your string holes, remembering that you have two holes in each hand for the acrobat on sticks and stand (shown in fig. 1A), and only one hole in each hand for the acrobat on bars, fig. 1B. Now you can cut around your surround line, and you should have a piece of tracing paper the same size as your plywood, 3½in×3in. Then pencil the reverse side of the tracing paper, and place on to your ⅛in plywood. By now, you will have learnt that it is much easier at this stage if you secure tape to all four corners of the workpiece, while you transfer the outline on to plywood.

2 Next, drill ten string holes for the acrobats on sticks and stand, marked 'C' in fig. 1, using a ⅟₁₆in drill. For the acrobat on bars, drill eight ⅟₁₆in holes, marked 'D' in fig. 1. In the centre of each hand, drill a ³⁄₁₆in hole, marked 'E' on fig. 1B, through which the bar will go. Taking your trusty hand fretsaw, cut out your five pieces of your acrobat figure, and glasspaper them smooth.

3 Paint and varnish all the pieces on both sides. A nice smile on the faces, please, and bright colours for all the various limbs.

4 To assemble your acrobat figure, see fig. 2. Firstly, clean out all the string holes and make sure that they are free from all paint and varnish. Then take one piece of string, 2in long, and tie a double knot at one end. Transfer your gaze to fig. 2, to solve a little knotty problem! Just thread the string through one of the acrobat's little legs, commencing at point A, and go through the hole in the lower half of the body, and out through the second leg, finishing at point B. Then immediately tie a double knot, but don't tie it too tightly, because you will want plenty of free movement of the limbs. Having done this, continue the same procedure with the arms. Then, having completed this simple task, cut off the waist string (shown in fig. 2c) and glue the knot to secure.

Put the little fellow away safely, until you have made either your sticks, stand or bars. He will look pretty helpless lying there, but once you have completed the next stage of assembly, be assured that he will spring into life and movement with great alacrity!

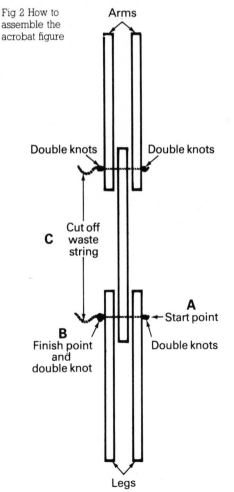

Fig 2 How to assemble the acrobat figure

Arms

Double knots   Double knots

C   Cut off waste string

A ← Start point

B
Finish point and double knot

Double knots

Legs

Materials
1 piece ⅛in plywood, 3½in×3in
2 pieces string, each 2in long × ⅟₁₆in thick

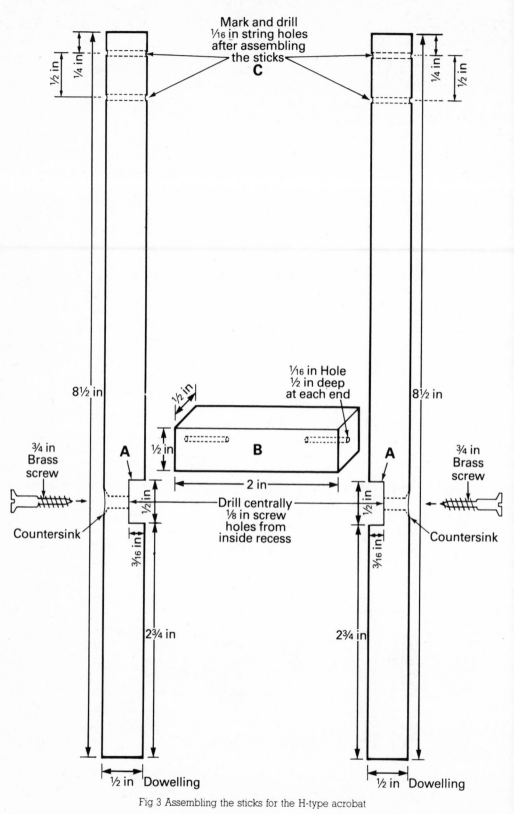

Mark and drill
1/16 in string holes
after assembling
the sticks
C

1/2 in   1/4 in

8½ in

1/16 in Hole
½ in deep
at each end

¾ in
Brass
screw

½ in

A   ½ in   **B**   **A**

½ in

¾ in
Brass
screw

Countersink

Drill centrally
1/8 in screw
holes from
inside recess

2 in

3/16 in

2¾ in   2¾ in

Countersink

3/16 in

½ in Dowelling   ½ in Dowelling

Fig 3 Assembling the sticks for the H-type acrobat

STICKS FOR H-TYPE ACROBAT
Method

1 Take your two lengths of ½in×8½in dowelling and following the plan in fig. 3 mark out the position of the crossbar. Measure from the ends of the dowelling 2¾in and then ½in. The string holes are marked and drilled after the sticks are assembled. Now, take your hand fretsaw, and cut out the recesses (shown shaded in fig. 3A), to a depth of 3/16in. Remember to cut to the insides of the lines, because these will be the recesses where your crossbar will fit. Having done this, drill an ⅛in hole in the centre of the recesses, and out again through the other side. Then, countersink your hole on the opposite side of the recesses. For those of you who do not possess a countersink bit, don't worry. You can use instead a ¼in drill. If you do, go carefully and don't drill too deeply – just deeply enough for your screwhead to fit snugly so that no one catches their hands on projecting screwheads.

Take your crossbar (shown in fig. 3B) and drill a 1/16in hole centrally in each end of this bar to a depth of approximately ½in; you don't need to be too exact with this hole depth. This acts as a pilot hole for your screw.

2 And now to assemble the sticks. Put a little wood glue around one recess only – it doesn't matter which one that you choose first – and then fit the crossbar into the recesses, and secure together with your two brass screws, using a screwdriver. Having done this, you can now mark and drill your 1/16in string holes through the sides of the sticks, to the measurements shown in fig. 3c. Now you may give the sticks a good glasspapering and varnishing afterwards. That completes the first set of sticks for the acrobat – the H type.

Materials
2 lengths ½in dowelling 8½in long
2 countersink brass wood screws ¾in
  (size 4s)
1 length ½in × ½in square ramin 2in long

STICKS FOR JAPANESE ACROBAT
Method

1 Take your cane and measure the string holes, as shown in fig. 4. Drill your 1/16in holes. To bend the cane to the desired U shape, all you have to do is get a piece of cloth and wind this around the centre of the piece of cane. Soak the cloth well with water, and this in turn will soak into the cane piece. After an hour, remove the cloth, and gently bend your cane. You can wind it round a rolling-pin, but don't bend the cane too much – the required shape is shown in fig. 4B. Then tie a string across to hold the cane in the desired position. Glasspaper the cane when thoroughly dry.

Fig. 4A shows just how the cane looks when you have assembled the acrobat within it – the instructions for doing this are given in the 'assembly' paragraphs (page 67). Do not varnish the cane as it will lose its elastic properties.

Materials
1 length strong pliable cane, having plenty of spring, 16in long and about ½in thick

---

STAND
Method

1 Take your 5in×4in×1in hardwood block, which will be the base for your stand, and mark out the positions of all your holes by following the plan shown in fig. 5, starting with a centre line. Having done this, drill your two ¼in holes first, as shown in fig. 5A, followed by your two ½in holes, shown in fig. 5B, all to a depth of ¾in. Now take your ¼in wood chisel, and carefully cut out the waste wood, shown shaded in fig. 5C, and finish off with a hole measuring ¾in×½in× ¾in deep, shown in fig. 5D. Next, drill your 1/16in hole in the side of your block (see fig. 5E) inwards, towards the centre, which will emerge at the hole shown in fig. 5D. Having done this, chamfer your base, and glasspaper it.

61

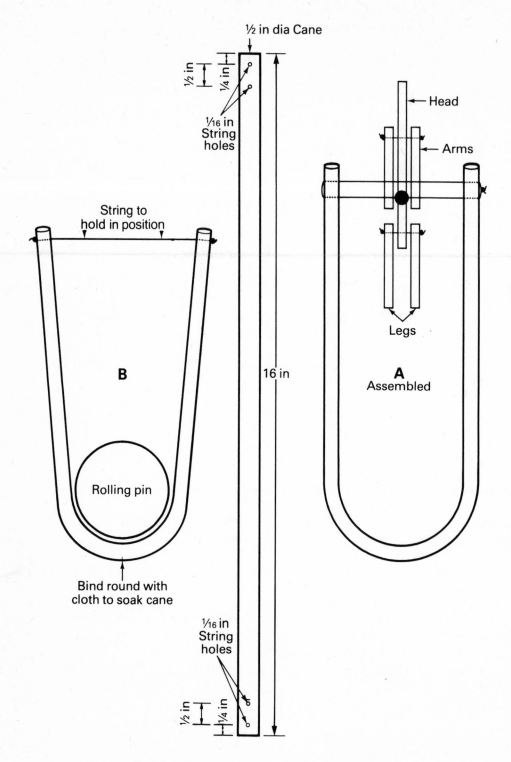

½ in dia Cane

½ in
¼ in
1/16 in String holes

Head

Arms

String to hold in position

B

16 in

Legs

A
Assembled

Rolling pin

Bind round with cloth to soak cane

1/16 in String holes

½ in
¼ in

Fig 4 Assembling the sticks for the Japanese acrobat

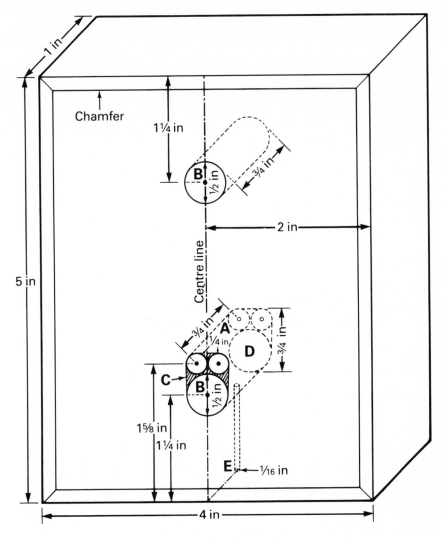

Fig 5 Hardwood base of the stand

2 Now for your two ½in dowellings. These are to be your uprights. Mark out as shown in fig. 6. Start with your ¾in; don't mark your string holes in yet. Take one of your dowellings, and cut a piece out to a ¼in depth, shown in the shaded part of fig. 6A. Now take your hardwood base, and place the dowelling as shown in fig. 6B, into your ¾in×½in× ¾in deep hole (shown in fig. 6C). Using a ¹⁄₁₆in drill bit, push through the hole in the base of fig. 6D, and mark the position of the hole on to your dowelling, as shown in fig. 6E. Remove the dowel, then proceed to drill a ³⁄₃₂in hole at the point you have marked.

3 All that remains now is the crossbar, which is your 4in×1½in×½in hardwood block. Don't forget to draw your centre line, and then mark out as shown in fig. 7. Drill your two ½in holes through the block. When you are doing this, rest your hardwood block on a piece of scrap wood, to prevent splintering around the holes on the reverse side. Radius the corners of your crossbar by using your hand fretsaw, and chamfer the top and bottom edges all around. Then, glasspaper. 4 Now to assemble your stand. Follow the plan shown in fig. 8. First, put a little wood glue on one dowelling only, at the position

63

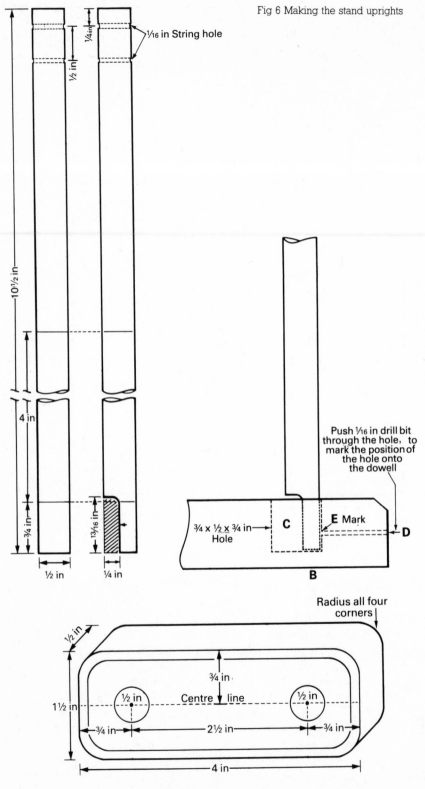

Fig 6 Making the stand uprights

¹⁄₄ in

½ in

¹⁄₁₆ in String hole

10½ in

4 in

¾ in

¹³⁄₁₆ in

½ in

¼ in

Push ¹⁄₁₆ in drill bit through the hole, to mark the position of the hole onto the dowell

¾ x ½ x ¾ in Hole

C

E Mark

D

B

Radius all four corners

½ in

¾ in

½ in

Centre line

½ in

1½ in

¾ in

2½ in

¾ in

4 in

Fig 7 Hardwood crossbar

64

shown in fig. 8A. Also put a little wood glue into your ½in hole in the base (shown in fig. 8B). Next, push your crossbar on to your two dowellings, to the lines marked in fig. 8C. Having done this, fit your dowellings into their respective holes, until they reach the full depth of the holes in the base. Take your 2¼in long brass rod, and form a loop at one end (see fig. 8D), using a small pair of pliers. Fit this by pushing it into the hole in the base (shown in fig. 8E), then out through the hole in the dowelling (fig. 8F), until the hook of the rod rests against the side of the base. And now for your final holes.

Firstly mark and drill two ⅟₁₆in holes, using the measurements given in fig. 8G, into the side of your crossbar, then on through into your dowelling to a depth of 1⅛in. Gently hammer your 1¼in brass rods (fig. 8H) into each hole, until the rods are flush with your crossbar. And, finally, you can drill your ⅟₁₆in string holes. Measurements for this are clearly given in fig. 6. Now glasspaper and varnish thoroughly.

Note. If you are making this stand for anyone who wants to use it as a therapeutic device, ie to strengthen their grip, remove the 2¼in brass rod from the base, just enough to fit a spring of your choice (fig. 8I), then replace the rod. This spring will give more tension to the acrobat stand. As muscular power develops in the hand grip, then a stronger spring may be introduced in the same way at a later date. This version is particularly apt for many stroke victims, whose hand muscles over a period of time will gradually grow stronger with regular hand exercises. And what is more, the acrobat on stand is so much more interesting than the usual rubber ball used in regular therapy!

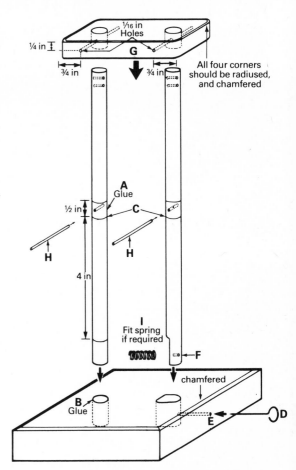

Fig 8 Assembly of stand (not to scale)

BARS FOR ACROBAT
Method

1 Mark out your 5in×4in×1in hardwood base, as shown in fig. 9. Drill your two ½in holes to a depth of ¾in. Now you can chamfer your block, and glasspaper. Next, put a little wood glue around each of the holes in the base. Push in your ½in dowelling, until you reach the full depth of the hole. Now mark out and drill in the top of each dowelling a ¹³⁄₆₄in hole. Measure your distance from the base upwards, as shown in fig. 9, making sure that you drill squarely, because your crossbar, 4in piece of dowelling, (see fig 9A) has to fit and turn easily. Glue and fit one of your beads to the end of your crossbar, as shown in fig. 9B. Glasspaper this and varnish.

Materials
1 piece hardwood, 5in×4in×1in
2 lengths ½in dowelling 10½in long
1 piece hardwood, 4in×1½in×½in
1 brass rod, 2¼in long × ⅟₁₆in thick
2 brass rods, 1¼in long × ⅟₁₆in thick
springs (optional)

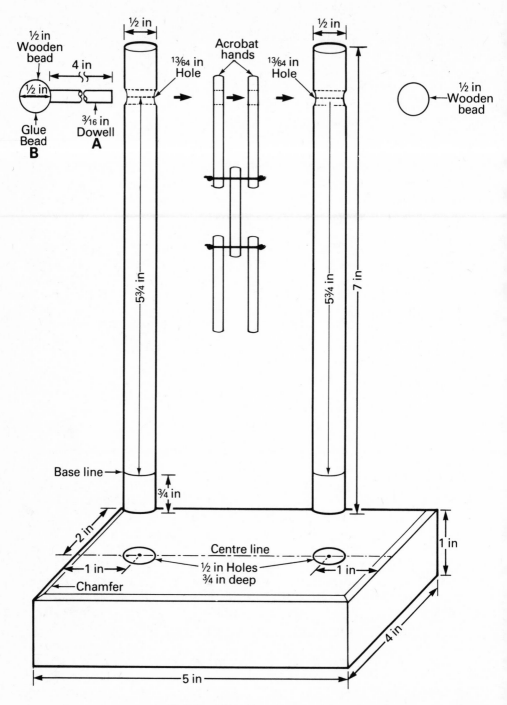

Fig 9 Assembly of bars (not to scale)

2 To assemble your acrobat on bars, ensure that the hand holes are clear of all paint and varnish. Then follow the plan shown in fig. 9. Push your crossbar through the first piece of dowelling, then through the hands of the acrobat, and out through the second dowelling. Then fit your remaining bead, using a little wood glue to secure it. Position the acrobat's hands centrally, and mark the position on the bar. Move the acrobat's hands to one side, and put a little wood glue around the bar, at the position marked. Reposition the acrobat's hands onto the glue. And, when all is completely dry, give the beads a little twist, and watch him perform!

Materials
1 piece hardwood, 5in×4in×1in
2 lengths ½in dowelling 7in long
1 length ³⁄₁₆in dowelling 4in long
two ½in wooden beads

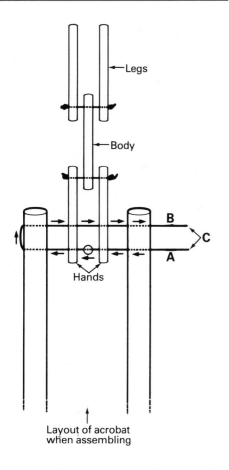

Legs

Body

B
C
A

Hands

Layout of acrobat
when assembling

ASSEMBLING
Method
Follow the plan in fig. 10 – it's easy. Taking your piece of string, and starting at point A, thread through the lower hole of your first upright, then through the top hole in the hand; position the wooden bead between the hands and pass the string through it, go on through the second hand, and out through the hole in the second upright; thread back through the remaining holes, in reverse sequence, and finish at point B. Now tie a triple knot at the end of your string (shown at 10c). Trim off the loose ends of the string, and glue the knot. And now for the moment of truth – the testing time. Place your stand on a table, or hold your sticks in an upright position, and the figure will hang as shown in fig. 10c. For sticks for Japanese acrobat, see fig. 4A. Give a sharp squeeze at the lower end of the sticks and the string will straighten out and propel your acrobat up and over. For the Japanese version, gently squeeze the sticks inwards; this motion will then twist the strings sufficiently for the cane to spring outwards, sending your acrobat up and over.

Materials
1 length string, 10in long × ¹⁄₁₆in thick
one ⅛in wooden bead

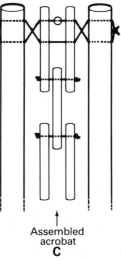

Assembled
acrobat
C

Fig 10 Assembly of
sticks (not to scale)

10 Acrobat on Platform

Colour plate 5

This toy was created specially for the younger child, who saw his older brother or sister playing with an acrobat on sticks, but was unable to use the toy himself. We adapted and modified this folk toy from one that has been around for a long, long time. It achieved prominence in the Victorian era – 'the Monkey up a stick'. This is a monkey figure, with jointed arms and legs which are pinned to a small hollow rod. When this rod is pushed up a stick within the rod, the monkey climbs with it to the top of the stick, where it flips up and over in a very pleasing manner. Other variations include acrobatically inclined performing cats, dogs and chimpanzees. There is also a similar model that we have seen in a toy museum, depicting a bear. This is of Russian origin. Our version has a clown performing displays of agile acrobatics, which can also be worked upside down and sideways. It is suitable for handicapped as well as for very young children, because it can be worked using one hand only: to lift and let fall.

Many adults enjoy them, but, after talking and listening to many mothers of younger children, we definitely think that this toy is an innovatory plaything for both babies, and also for younger children up to two and a half. After all, for thousands of years the toy range for children of these tender years was very limited, and restricted in the main to the toy rattle. This was, in its original form, probably just a dried nut, whose seeds rattled inside and gave out a pleasant noise when shaken. Even today, baby rattles tend usually to operate on exactly the same principle, although now of course these seeds have been superseded (no pun intended) by bells or balls in the interior of the rattles. The only other moving folk toy for very young ones that we can think of is the old cup-and-stick toy. This is a cone of wood, shaped rather like an ice-cream cornet, and when the child pushes up a rod inside this, a jazzily dressed Mr Punch–type clown immediately emerges, waving his arms. The acrobat on platform, however, exerts a powerful influence upon even the youngest child, because he can make the clown perform himself.

Method

1 Now that you have made one, or all of our Freds, or acrobats on sticks, stand or bars, you can now go on to make the son of Fred, as we call the acrobat on platform.

To start; again, do not cut your tracing paper to size at this stage, as you could find it a little difficult to hold and to trace. So take your full piece of tracing paper and place on the acrobat illustrations (figs 1A and 1B). Trace out the four limbs and the body, not forgetting the surround lines and your drill holes. Now you can cut out your tracing paper: just cut around the black border. Pencil the reverse side of both pieces of tracing paper. Then tape these down on your plywood – remembering that the ⅛in thick plywood is for the limbs of the acrobat, and the ¼in thick plywood is for the body.

2 Drill your ⅛in holes in the limbs, and ⁵⁄₃₂ holes in the body. And now, take up your hand fretsaw, and cut out all your pieces; then you can glasspaper these.

3 Paint and varnish on all sides, brightness, boldness and gaiety being the three key-notes here.

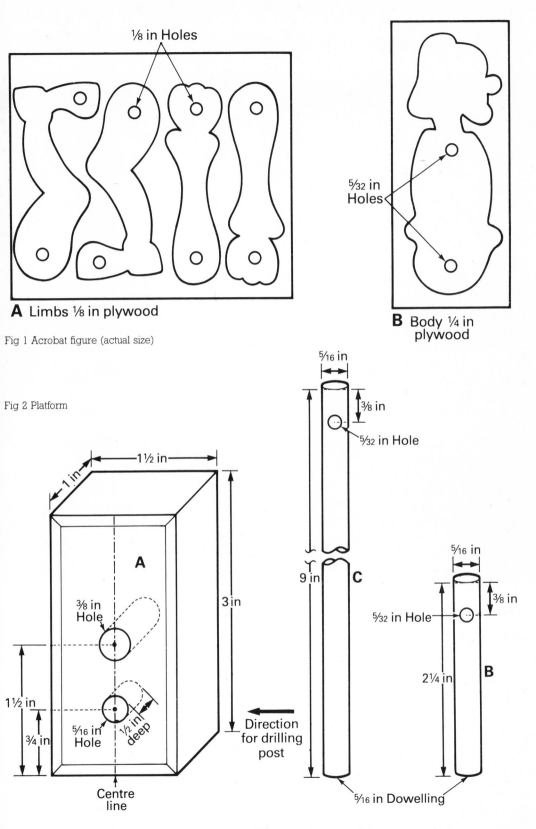

¹⁄₈ in Holes

A Limbs ¹⁄₈ in plywood

Fig 1 Acrobat figure (actual size)

B Body ¼ in plywood

⁵⁄₃₂ in Holes

Fig 2 Platform

⁵⁄₁₆ in

³⁄₈ in

⁵⁄₃₂ in Hole

1½ in

1 in

³⁄₈ in Hole

A

3 in

9 in **C**

⁵⁄₁₆ in

³⁄₈ in

⁵⁄₃₂ in Hole

2¼ in **B**

1½ in

⁵⁄₁₆ in Hole

½ in deep

¾ in

Direction for drilling post

Centre line

⁵⁄₁₆ in Dowelling

69

4 Take your hardwood block, which will be your platform. Mark out the position of your holes, as shown in fig. 2A. Next, drill your ⁵⁄₁₆in hole, to a depth of ½in. Then drill your ³⁄₈in hole through the stand. Again, when doing this operation, make sure that you rest your stand on some waste wood to prevent splintering around the hole on the reverse side. You can now chamfer the edges of the platform, and glasspaper this. Put a little wood glue around the ⁵⁄₁₆in hole in your platform. Then take your 2¼in dowelling (see fig. 2B) and push it firmly into the hole. This will be the post for your acrobat's hand to pivot upon. Mark the position and drill a ⁵⁄₃₂in hole in the post and the push rod, to the measurements given in figs. 2B and 2C. When drilling the post, drill in the direction of the arrow, from the side. Now, with your pencil sharpener, remove the edges of the ends of the dowellings; all that remains to be done now is to varnish the platform, in preparation for assembly.

5 Assembly time once again. Take the acrobat's arms and legs, and put a little wood glue in each one of your holes. Then take your four pieces of ⅛in dowelling, ⅝in long, and push these into one set of limbs, as shown in fig. 3A, making sure that you place the limbs all on a clean, flat surface. Next, give the holes in the body of your acrobat a good clean out, because we want him, once assembled, to move easily, cleanly and well. Now to assemble.

Following the illustration in fig. 3, put your push rod on to dowelling B, and the lower hole in the acrobat's body to dowelling C. Then place the second leg on to the dowelling, and very gently, using a small hammer, tap them together, until the dowelling is flush with the legs. Now put your push rod through the ³⁄₈in hole in the platform.

Now to fit the arms. Push dowelling D through the hole in the top half of the body, and the dowelling on hand (E) through the hole in the post. Then place the remaining arm on your dowelling, and again, using your hammer, gently tap until your dowelling is flush with the surface. Don't get impatient. Wait for the glue to dry thoroughly before giving him his first work-out. Just hold the block upright and push and pull the rod, and the acrobat performs a super range of gymnastics. He can also work sideways, and upside down, and can even be used by a little child single-handed.

If you wish to make a proper job of completing your acrobat on platform, don't forget to 'touch in' with paint the bare wood of the dowelling edges on his limbs.

And now, you have created another stunning moving folk toy.

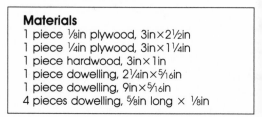

Materials
1 piece ⅛in plywood, 3in×2½in
1 piece ¼in plywood, 3in×1¼in
1 piece hardwood, 3in×1in
1 piece dowelling, 2¼in×⁵⁄₁₆in
1 piece dowelling, 9in×⁵⁄₁₆in
4 pieces dowelling, ⅝in long × ⅛in

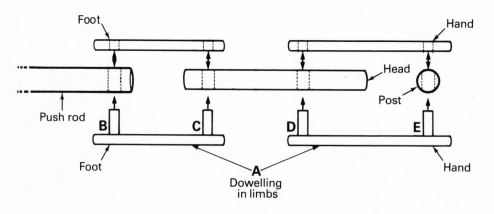

Fig 3 Assembling the acrobat

11 Pecking Birds

Colour plate 5

This wonderful toy came from eastern Europe many centuries ago. It has changed very little in concept and design through the years. Birds of many kinds and chickens have usually been used, because, in many parts of the world, birds are regarded as fertility symbols. Also, the shape of their bodies lends itself quite naturally to the idea of 'pecking' for their food. The simplest version of this classically moving folk toy that we have seen is just one chicken pecking on a small board. At the opposite end of the scale, the deluxe version is one man feeding grain to three free-range chicks, while a fourth chick pecks for his food from between the bars of a small cage. A well-known Victorian version has a single bird pecking, which is clamped to a table and moved manually by setting in motion a weighted pendulum swinging freely beneath the bird.

Literally hundreds of people have told us about (what we have come to call) the 'prisoner of war pecking bird'. During World War II, thousands of German and Italian prisoners of war were brought to England, and many were sent into rural areas to help out on the farms. Young English male farm workers were absent, serving in the armed forces at home and abroad at that time. In spite of having a splendidly capable group of ladies working on the land (known as the Land Army Girls), lack of mechanisation meant that there were heavy manual tasks to be performed, suited to the stronger men; hence the need for prisoner-of-war labour. Many of these young prisoners made the pecking-bird toy, which they sold, or bartered for food and cigarettes with the local populace. The birds were in great demand, as the local children found them irresistibly appealing. The prisoners fashioned the pecking birds from scrap wood, using baling cord, and odd bits and bobs. They even managed to decorate them. Having no access to paint, they used thin wire, which they heated over a fire, then pyrographed patterns on to the birds. Although so many people remember having a set of these birds as a child, not one that we know of survives now. So, if you have one, keep it safely, as this plaything is now a rare and historical curiosity.

Disabled children also take a delight in these toys, for to swing the handle of the board around and to see the chickens peck for food is a great delight.

There are many other ideas for you to use, apart from the birds. You can also create washer-ladies with washtubs, blacksmiths and their anvils, drummer boys, footballers and cancan dancers.

You have already read about the Russian, German and Italian versions of this plaything; now comes the Cornish creation of the pecking bird! Slightly lower in the pecking order of things, we might add. However, get the birdseed ready, and here we go!

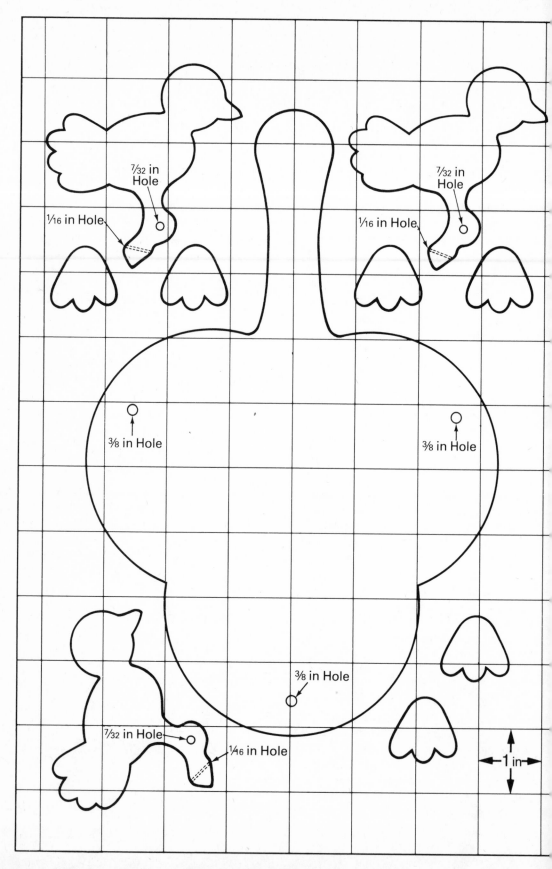

Fig 1 Layout of pecking birds (not to scale)

Method

1 Here, there is a slight variation on the usual procedure. Take a piece of tracing paper and draw a grid with each square representing 1in. Then follow the line illustration shown in fig. 1. Draw one bird, one foot and one base to scale – don't forget your drill holes. Take a sharp pair of scissors and cut round the outlines to make your patterns. Then pencil the positions of the drill holes onto the reverse side of the tracing paper patterns. Place the patterns flat on to your piece of ¼in plywood – hold steady and, using your pencil, carefully draw around the patterns to make one base, three birdies and six footsies. Once again, remember to mark in the drill holes.

2 Next, drill all your holes marked ⅜in in the base, and ⁷⁄₃₂in in the birds. Having done this, take your hand fretsaw and cut out your ten sections. You will now require a ¹⁄₁₆in hole in each foot, in the position and direction shown. This is where you will later tie the string which will secure the ball or pendulum beneath the board. Then glasspaper, paying special attention to the edges, especially the handle of the base, to avoid splinters.

3 Now, you can paint the sides of the birds. Perhaps a cheery tit, robin and finch will be pleasant. Then the sides and top *only* of the six feet. And also, paint a circle in the centre of the base, complete with seed – easily done by plopping down bright dots within the radius of your solidly painted surface of the circle. When the paint is dry, glue the feet to the base, in pairs. To do this, just smear a little wood glue on to the bottom of the feet, and place firmly on to the base, as shown in fig. 2A. When all is dry, you can then varnish all you have painted so far, including the base.

4 Take your ³⁄₁₆in dowelling, 3in long, which is going to be your hinge bar on which the pecking birds will pivot. First, mark out the positions shown in fig. 3A and, at the points marked, drill a ¹⁄₁₆in hole. This will allow your gimp pins to enter. If you do not drill these holes, you will split the dowelling. Having done this, you can glasspaper, paint and varnish. When all is completely dry, mark out your 1in sections, as shown in fig. 3B, and cut to the length that you have marked, using your hand fretsaw. Take a piece of glasspaper, and gently rub off the burrs. Then paint the ends.

5 Fit your lead weight into your 1¼in wooden ball. To do this, drill a ½in hole to a depth of ¾in in the centre of the ball. Then place your lead weight into the hole shown in fig 4A. To cap the hole, use a piece of ½in dowelling, and glue this into the hole shown in fig. 4B. When the glue has dried, trim this dowelling flush with the surface of the ball, using your hand fretsaw. And then glasspaper. Now, drill your ⅛in hole into the ball, approximately ½in deep, as shown in fig. 4B. Having done this, you can now proceed to paint the ball. The most effective-looking balls are those of contrasting colours, so

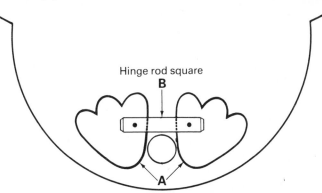

Fig 2 Position of feet on base

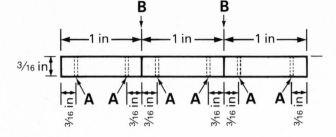

B   B

|← 1 in →|← 1 in →|← 1 in →|

3/16 in

3/16 in   A   A   3/16 in 3/16 in   A   A   3/16 in 3/16 in   A   A   3/16 in

Fig 3 Hinge bar

Fig 4 Fitting the lead weight into the wooden ball

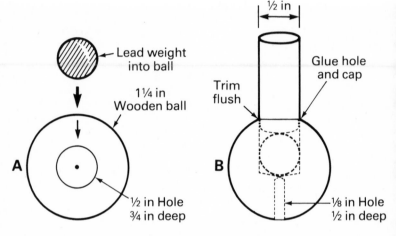

Lead weight into ball

1¼ in Wooden ball

A

½ in Hole
¾ in deep

½ in

Glue hole and cap

Trim flush

B

⅛ in Hole
½ in deep

you could have a deep bold solidly painted background, and then use a thinner brush to paint slimmer brush strokes outwards, radiating from the top of the ball. Or you could paint large dots on your ball, or pretty star-shaped patterns to make your ball stand out strikingly – like a fiery racing comet in a dark night in the heavens.

6 Now is the time to assemble your pretty little birdies. First of all, clean out all the string holes and bar holes of paint and varnish. Follow the assembly plan in fig. 5. Take one piece of your 8in long piece of string, and tie a double knot at one end; thread this through the string hole in the foot, shown in fig 5A. Then, using the 1in hinge bar (fig. 3), push this through the 7/32in hole in the foot, and fix to the feet on the base. Do this, by using two ½in gimp pins, and gently tap them through your pilot hole in the hinge bar, and then on, into the feet, as shown in fig. 5B. Making sure that the bar is square to the edge of the base, illustrated in fig. 2B, continue with this same procedure in re-

spect of the other two birds. Having done this, push your loose ends of the string through the ⅜in hole, shown in fig. 5c. Rest the pecking birds upside down on a flat surface. Hold and gather all the strings upwards, together, making sure that they are all equal in length, and tie a knot (as shown in fig. 5D). Now, put a little glue into the ⅛in hole in your weighted ball (see fig. 5E) and, finally, push the knotted string into the full depth of the hole. Pick up the base by the handle, letting the ball hang down beneath the base, and gently rotate the board. Then, the little dicky birds will peck away so very merrily for you.

Materials
1 piece ¼in plywood, 10in×8in
1 length 3/16in dowelling 3in long
one ½in lead weight
one 1¼in wooden ball
3 pieces string, 8in long × 1/16in thick
six ½in gimp pins
1 piece dowelling, ½in thick × not less than ½in long

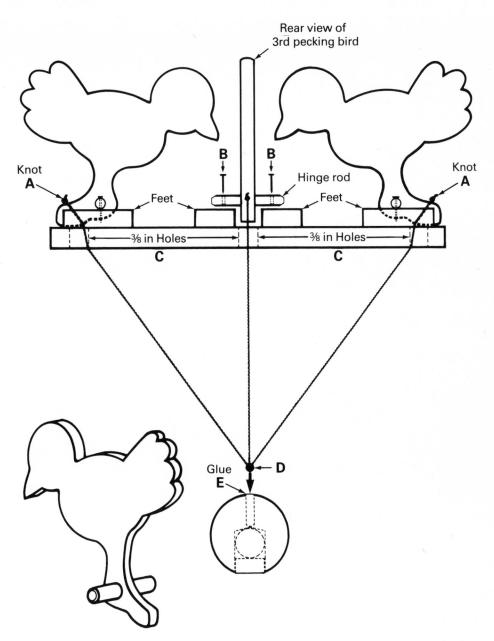

Rear view of
3rd pecking bird

Knot
A

B **B**

Hinge rod

Feet

Feet

Knot
A

3/8 in Holes

3/8 in Holes

C

C

Glue

D

E

Fig 5 How to assemble the pecking birds; the inset illustration shows one bird with hinge bar in position

12 The Merry-go-round
Colour plate 6

The merry-go-round, or carousel, was originally a device used to train young warriors in the art of tilting. This contraption consisted of a series of weighted pads suspended from rotating arms that radiated outwards from a fixed central pole. The young men, mounted on horseback, aimed their lances at the centre of a pad – the 'Bull's Eye'. If they hit the target anywhere but at dead centre, they would be fetched a hefty clout on the head swiftly from the next swinging pad on the carousel, so they presumably soon learned to 'hit their mark' or to be 'spot on' the mark. In seventeenth-century Europe, the idea developed of suspending carved horses from extended poles, and so the first carousel, used for peaceful purposes, was born. Later, the invention of steam power, the stationary engine, and the flat belt drive helped to produce the merry-go-round of the fairground that is known and loved today. We also owe a great debt to the men who carved and painted the animals of the carousel: Gustav Sentzel from Germany, Frank Caretta from Milan and Salvatore Cernigliaro from Palermo. Many of their bright baroque designs inspired later toymakers to produce beautifully fashioned and boldly painted clockwork carousel automata.

Our own simple merry-go-round we accredit entirely to the unknown lady, whom we met in Truro City Hall many years ago. We were selling our toys there at a craft show when she came up to us and asked us if we sold the merry-go-round. 'Which merry-go-round would that be?' we asked, intensely interested. 'My grandfather used to make them for all the children of the family,' she replied, 'but even Harrods doesn't stock them.' She then proceeded to draw a diagram of how this merry-go-round worked. We had never previously seen this version, or read or heard of it. And when we actually came to make our first carousel, and we saw just how well and effectively it worked, it quite exceeded our expectations. We therefore owe a great debt of gratitude to this lady.

Some of the most popular themes that we have incorporated into our merry-go-rounds have been 'Hey Diddle Diddle', 'The Owl and the Pussycat', as well as various circus themes. There are, of course, endless variations. What about 'Baa Baa Black Sheep', a horse race, or even one of our magnificent 'Tinker, tailor, soldier, sailor, rich man, poor man, beggarman, thief' merry-go-rounds? We have found that everyone loves a merry-go-round. Babies are simply hypnotised by the colour and the continuous movement, which can stop tears immediately in most babies. Younger children spin them all day long. Adults can use them on the office desk or by the telephone, or as a dinner-table centrepiece. We even had one chap who bought some as centrepieces for all the dining-tables in his restaurant. And he sold these quickly to all his customers – and came back for more! Now, best of all, disabled children find these merry-go-rounds easy to move and to use.

Whenever we have them at a craft show or exhibition, and set them all in motion, children, as well as full-grown men and women just stand, staring in amazement at the movements.

The Owl and the Pussycat

The owl and the pussycat went to sea
In a beautiful pea-green boat.
They took some honey, and plenty of
    money
Wrapped up in a five pound note.
The owl looked up to the stars above
And sang to a small guitar,
'O lovely pussy! O pussy, my love.
What a beautiful pussy you are'.
They sailed away for a year and a day
To the land where the bong-tree grows.
And there in a wood a piggy-wig stood
With a ring at the end of his nose.
'Dear pig, are you willing to sell for one
    shilling
Your ring?' Said the piggy, 'I will'.
So they took it away, and were married
    next day
By the turkey who lives on the hill.
They dined on mince and slices of quince
Which they ate with a runcible spoon.
And hand in hand, on the edge of the
    sand,
They danced by the light of the moon,
The moon, they danced by the light of the
    moon.

                                    Edward Lear

Hey Diddle Diddle

Sing hey diddle diddle
The cat and the fiddle
The cow jumped over the moon.
The little dog laughed to see such fun
And the dish ran away with the spoon.

                                    (Traditional)

The Circus

Come to the circus,
We'll show you around.
Come see the circus merry-go-round.

Ringmaster cracks his whip,
And the show's under way.
The clown entertains you,
All happy and gay.

The elephants enter.
The spotlight reveals
Music and laughter
And performing seals!

                                    J. L. Peduzzi

ONE MERRY-GO-ROUND AND ONE SET OF FIGURES

Method

1 Take your tracing paper, and draw a $10\frac{1}{2}$in $\times$ 4in box section, but do not cut out. Now choose the set of merry-go-round figures that you wish to make, shown in figs 1A, 1B and 1c. Begin to trace out your set of figure shapes at the positions shown on the layout plan, but do keep within your box section. And now, take your scissors and cut out the box that you have marked round. Back once again to the old routine of pencilling the reverse side of your tracing paper, and placing this on to your piece of $\frac{1}{4}$in plywood, $10\frac{1}{2}$in $\times$ 4in. Tape the four corners down to keep your work steady. And, using your pencil, transfer the outlines of your four figures to your plywood.

2 Take your second piece of $\frac{1}{4}$in $\times$ $10\frac{1}{2}$in $\times$ 4in plywood, and spread a little wood glue over the whole surface. Having done this, place your first piece of plywood, with the figures traced out and facing outwards, on top of this, and glue them together, making sure that all the sides are flush.

Now take your $\frac{1}{2}$in gimp pin, and nail together at the points shown on the layout plans. You may say, why do this? We are using $\frac{1}{4}$in plywood for most of the projects within this book, so, if you stick two $\frac{1}{4}$in pieces together, it is less expensive than to go out and buy a piece of $\frac{1}{2}$in plywood. We do like to think of everyone's pockets. When all is dry, take up your fretsaw, and cut out the figures; all four of these. Take your time doing this, because there are some ins and outs, and corners and angles. If you are making the owl and the pussycat carousel, when you come to the owl and pussy in their ship, fig. 1A, cut between the sail and the mast, at point c, to remove the section of wood between the head of the owl and the cat's head. When you have done this, you can now glasspaper all four figures.

3 Now drill a $\frac{3}{16}$in hole in the base of each figure to a depth of $\frac{1}{2}$in, as shown in the layout plans, figs. 2A, 2B and 2C.

(instructions continue on page 82)

77

Fig 1A 'The owl and the pussycat' figures (actual size)

Fig 1B 'Hey diddle diddle' figures (actual size)

Fig 1C Circus figures (actual size)

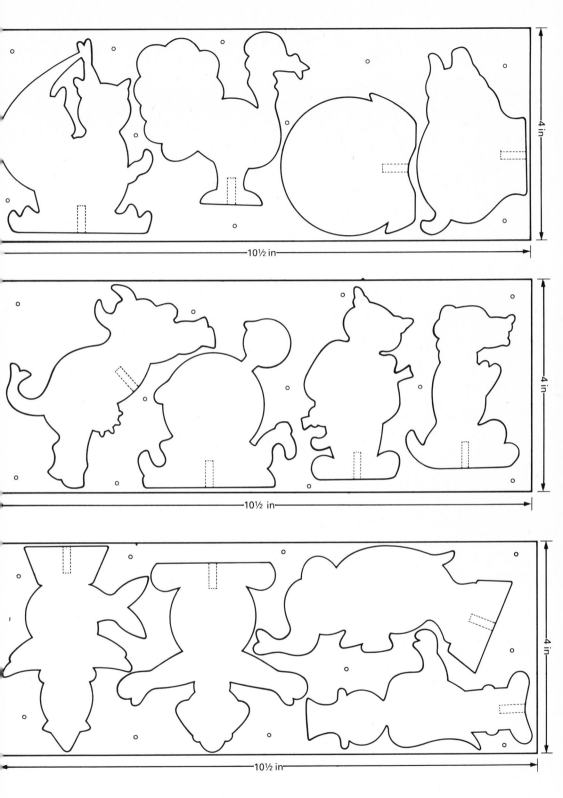

Fig 2A Layout plans (not to scale) showing positions of ³⁄₁₆in × ½in deep drill holes for pegs. Nail holes marked O. (*top*) The owl and the pussycat; (*centre*) Hey diddle diddle; (*bottom*) Circus

81

Having drilled a hole in the base of each figure, take your four pieces of 3/16in×1in dowelling and, using your pencil sharpener, remove the rough edges from the ends of these. The next step is to put a little wood glue inside the holes of your figures, and push in one piece of dowelling to the full depth of the hole. These will act as pegs to hold the figures in position: three on the platform and one on top of the ball.

4 Before you start painting the figures, it is a good idea to get yourself a piece of scrap wood, and drill four 3/16in holes about 1in apart on the top. This will then enable you to stand your figures on it while they dry out. Now, go ahead and paint the figures. As this is a very special toy, what about trying for a very special bit of painting? Nothing elaborate, just something neat and simple, but with charm. Do your best, anyhow. This is all any of us can ever hope to do! When dry, varnish the figures all over; top, back, front and sides.

5 Now for your platform. Take your piece of 1/4in plywood, 8in×8in. You can either use the shape that is illustrated in fig. 3, or indeed any shape that takes your fancy. Or you can just elect to make a simple circular platform. Whichever shape you choose, mark out and drill all your holes, as shown in fig. 3: a 1/2in hole in the centre, which will allow for your stand post to pass through, 3/16in holes for the pegs of your figures to fit into; and last, but never least, 3/32in holes for your ribbon. When you have done this, you can then cut out your shape, and glasspaper it smooth. Now you can paint the edge of the platform with a fancy pattern, or stripes, running as a border all along the thin edge. When the platform is dry, varnish it.

6 Take your piece of 6in×6in×1in hardwood. This will be the base for your stand, as shown in fig. 4A. Mark out a 2 3/4in radius circle on to your hardwood. Then drill a 3/8in hole in the centre of your circle, to a depth of 3/4in. Take your fretsaw, and cut out the base

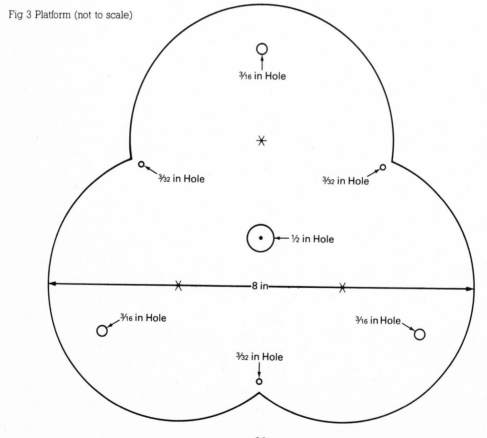

Fig 3 Platform (not to scale)

3/16 in Hole

*

3/32 in Hole   3/32 in Hole

1/2 in Hole

8 in

3/16 in Hole   3/16 in Hole

3/32 in Hole

for your stand. Then, once again, glass-paper. When you have done this, put a little wood glue around the inside of the hole in the base, and take your ⅜in×10½in dowelling, and push this into the full depth of the hole. Make sure that the dowelling is square to your base, otherwise you will have a wobbly merry-go-round. Then varnish, and you have now completed your stand.

7 The next step is to take your 1¼in wooden ball and, following the plan shown in fig. 4B, drill a ⅜in hole to a depth of ½in. Then drill a 9⁄16in hole in the opposite side of the wooden ball, emerging into the ½in hole. When performing this operation, do not hold the wooden ball in your hand. Always hold the ball securely in a vice (vise), or with a pair of pliers, remembering to cover the jaws. Glasspaper the edges of the hole, removing any rough bits.

Now take a piece of scrap wood, and drill a ⅜in hole. Insert into this hole a small piece of dowelling, the same size as your hole. Then insert the other end of the dowelling into your ball. In this way, you then have somewhere safe to place your ball for drying after painting it. Now paint your ball with a cheery little face on one or both sides, or use bright patterns. When it is dry, varnish it.

8 Now that all your painting and varnishing are completed, I think it would be a good idea at this stage to tell you how to assemble the merry-go-round. It's simple, and easy. Just follow the plan in fig. 5. First, take one length of your ribbon, and tie a double knot at one end, then thread the other end through your 3⁄32in hole shown in fig. 5A. Continue the same procedure with your two remaining ribbons.

You will need two little blocks of wood about 1½in high. Failing this, you can use two matchboxes. Place these on their sides, and then place them on to the base of your stand, at the points shown in fig. 5B. Take your platform, and slide it down over the centre dowelling, to rest on your blocks, or matchboxes. Take each ribbon in turn, and take them over the top of the dowelling, shown in fig. 5C. Hold them in position and, making sure that you have no slack in the ribbons, push your wooden ball on to the top of the dowelling, with just enough force to trap the ribbons. Then trim the loose ends of the ribbons; this is shown in fig. 5D. Push the

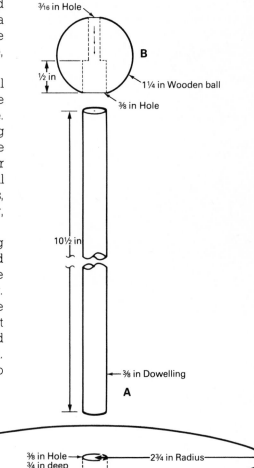

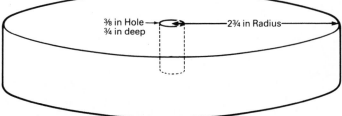

Fig 4 Merry-go-round stand and wooden bar

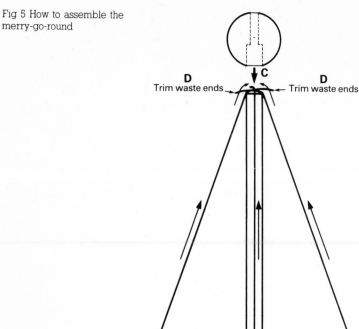

Fig 5 How to assemble the merry-go-round

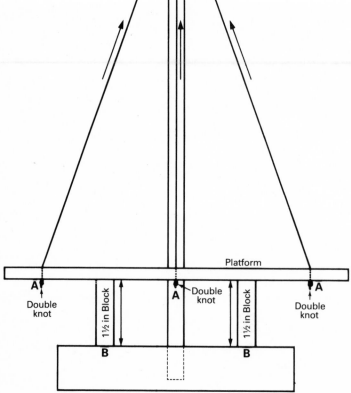

D Trim waste ends. — **C** — **D** Trim waste ends

Platform

A Double knot

A 1½ in Block

A Double knot

1½ in Block

A Double knot

B   **B**

wooden ball firmly on to the dowelling to the full depth of the hole. Next, place your figures on to the platform, by pushing the pegs firmly through the ³⁄₁₆in holes. And don't forget to insert the fourth figure on the top of the ball. Take your blocks, or match-boxes, away, give a slight push to the platform – or even a shove – and away the merry-go-round revolves, back and forth and back again, and on and on.

This toy will give so much pleasure to so many people throughout the coming years. And you will be so proud to know that you, yourself, have made this wondrous thing!

Materials

2 pieces ¼in plywood, 10½in×4in
ten ½in gimp pins, or eleven if doing 'Hey Diddle Diddle'
4 lengths ³⁄₁₆in dowelling 1in long
1 piece scrap wood, approx 5in long
1 piece ¼in plywood, 8in×8in
1 piece hardwood, 6in×6in×1in
1 length ³⁄₈in dowelling 10½in long
one 1¼in wooden ball
one small piece scrap wood
one small piece dowelling
3 lengths coloured ribbon, 12in×¼in wide
2 small blocks wood approx. 1½in high or 2 matchboxes

13 The Ziggy-Zaggy

Colour plate 7

These scintillating playthings are very hard to leave alone, once made. Like the ladder-man and the merry-go-rounds, they attract continually questing fingers, and not just from small children – so be warned! Some friends who run a large hotel have one of these toys hung on the wall – a very big one indeed. They say that they always know the time that late-returning guests arrive, because they can hear a series of loud clicks punctuated by barely suppressed giggles, from adults of both sexes! Anthony's father remembers these being sold at markets throughout England, over fifty years ago. Just how old they are, we have no idea. We did see one ziggy-zaggy toy that a customer showed us, which her own father had made for her, and her sisters and brothers. This was a sailor returning to his ship, which was situated at the bottom of the sea! We knew this because the board at the top was adorned with painted waves, while lower down were fishes, and even a mermaid!

We have been asked to design a wide variety of ziggy-zaggy toys on commission. There is an alphabet version, which is ideally suited for teaching reading and spelling. Twenty-six letters in turn are made to drop down a long board, and, on this one, you can even have your own version of vertical scrabble. There was a lady who wanted a Cornish miner, carrying his pick, descending into a pit. A beekeeper asked for a bee flying down from a flower into the beehive, and we were even asked for Hickory Dickory Dock. This theme is based on an old traditional nursery rhyme, which runs

Hickory Dickory Dock
The mouse ran up the clock
The clock struck one
The mouse ran down
Hickory dickory dock.

We were later asked by a lady, who shall remain nameless (to protect the guilty), to design a ziggy-zaggy toy involving a poor lost soul plunging down the board, where demons and hellfire waited to receive him. This was actually intended as a gift for a small child. We politely but firmly declined to carry out this particular commission. We couldn't actually believe our own ears, when she told us of her wishes. We knew of course that in medieval times, long before the advent of the printed word and free education being made available to poor people, miracle plays and puppet shows de-picting the struggle between good and evil had been enacted, for both children and adults. And we also knew that the Victorians were great ones for incorporating moral lessons into many of the toys, books and games for their children, but this lady of today, we thought, really was the limit, until we saw a toymaker's work on display. Amongst other painted wooden toys re-served exclusively for children was, pro-minently displayed, a corpse, wrapped in a winding sheet and laid in an open coffin. Anthony and I just stood and looked at one another, and then collapsed, and fell about laughing! However, dismiss both morals and the macabre from your minds as of now, for our versions of the ziggy-zaggy toys – the teddy bear and the hen that lays eggs – are not in the least bit sad, and display only a zany and super happiness!

Teddy Bear

Who would have thought that a single cartoon published in America in the early 1900s, would have been instrumental in giving a universal and unprecedented boost to the toymaking industry, and is indeed still influencing the business today. Nevertheless, this happens to be true. It all started at the turn of the century, when Berryman, a famous cartoonist, drew, and subsequently had published, a cartoon of President Theodore (Teddy) Roosevelt refusing the chance to shoot a bear cub while on a hunting expedition in Mississippi. As well as making the incumbent president extremely popular with many animal lovers, the sight of this picture also generated a smart bit of enterprise back in Brooklyn. Morris Michton, who sold hand-made toys, was inspired upon seeing it to cut out the shape of the bear shown in the picture, stuff it, create an endearing expression on its face and place it on view in his window, naming it 'Teddy's Bear'. Everyone wanted one, and the lad was in business! Later on, he actually wrote to the president, asking for formal permission to use his name for the bear. 'Why not?', he thought, 'the president can only say 'No'.' The president in fact said yes to this request, thinking no doubt that this idea could be a marvellous vote-catcher. And so began the meteoric rise of the Teddy Bear.

Mind you, there have been other famous bears. Winnie the Pooh, for one. What a bear *par excellence*, created by A. A. Milne! Who could resist a bear 'of very little brain' and one with a strong penchant for honey? Milne in his Pooh books was also responsible for one of the greatest inventions of modern times – that glorious game called 'Pooh sticks'.

Long ago, we were desperately trying to think of a new popular character to integrate into our range of moving folk toys. We needed something that would prove to be extremely popular immediately, and would appeal to everyone, young and old. It was then that our friends called on us, bringing with them their daughter, Rachel, a bright child. This little girl, aged ten, was a gem, with a mind as shiny as a polished button; spouting questions, expounding and expanding on her personal philosophy of life; profound, yet radiant, and clearly destined to become one of life's great thinkers. At one point in the conversation, she said to us, 'Bear in mind what I tell you, for you will never forget it.' And she was absolutely right! It wasn't forgotten, for the bear in mind soon became the bear on the drawing board, then on to the bear as toy and plaything. And, this is the result. A lovely bear ziggy zaggy that you can make. And, if you can bear it, we will go on now and tell you just how this is made . . .

Hen Laying Egg

In the past few years, many people who previously lived in the city or the suburb, moved out into the countryside, to become homesteaders. Heavily influenced also by reading books dealing with self-sufficiency and food production, they came from flat and house out to cottage and cabin, with land. One of the main factors binding countrymen and newcomers alike together, is a love of animals, and poultry in particular. There is no need for an alarm clock. If you need an early-morning call, just leave the window open and the local cockerel, called Cocky, will do the rest. Yes, everyone here loves all his animals, and our neighbour Fred is a good case in point. He loves his hens, and so do his family. They treat them all as friends, calling each hen by name. Nothing is too good for the birds. Ages ago, he came over to see us. He commissioned us to produce a ziggy-zaggy hen laying an egg, for his young son's birthday. Alan, his boy, is a conscientious poultry lad, virtually sleeping with the hens, and refusing to go off to school until he has said 'good morning' to each one, and checked that they are all in good health. So, in order to do a good job, and to gain personal experience in the making of the toy, we did research at the hen-house. I wonder how many people have found such marvellous fascination there, as we did. For instance, we had wondered why the hens didn't appear outside until shortly after lunch. Anthony swore that they were tired out, and having a long lie-in inside; but the real reason is of course that they usually do their egg-laying in the morning.

After the hen that lays eggs ziggy-zaggy was complete and had been delivered, we quickly forgot about him. Then, suddenly, we got a spate of requests for this version of the toy from many of our neighbours whose children had seen the original, and wanted one for themselves. We also had a visit from someone who lives close by, and had heard of the toy. He brought with him, and showed us another kind of moving folk toy. A solid hen that lays actual eggs – but that is another story . . .

And, from that day to this, this version of the ziggy-zaggy plaything has been a real favourite with city folk, as well as with country folk. We called the hen Henrietta, and the egg Egbert! You can also make more than one egg for your ziggy-zaggy board, which you may care to name Eggs Tra Ordinary, Eggs Trava Ganza; don't get Eggs Ited. We are sure that you can think of many more.

HEN LAYING EGG, AND TEDDY BEAR
Method
1 First, we will start with your ¼in piece of plywood, 3in×18in. This will be the board for your ziggy-zaggy. Follow the plan very carefully, as shown in fig. 1, and mark out all your hole positions for your pegs to fit into, by starting at fig. 1A, and working upwards, finishing with your string hole at point B. Now centre-punch all your marked hole positions; this will help to prevent your drill bit from wandering and to stay centre of the holes when you start drilling.

2 Drill all your sixteen ³⁄₁₆in peg holes, but don't forget when drilling to rest your board on some waste wood to prevent splintering around the holes on the reverse side. Finish with the ⅛in string hole at the top. Having done this, cut a radius on all four corners of the board using your hand fretsaw, as shown

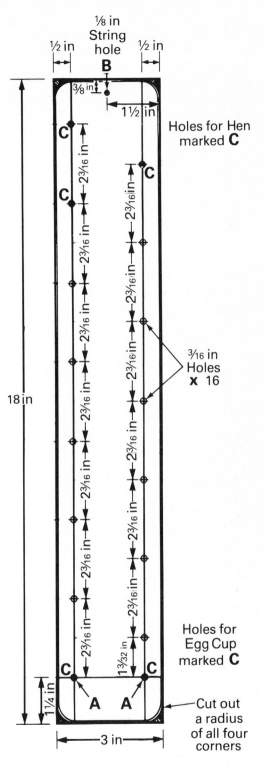

Fig 1 Ziggy-zaggy board, with peg positions marked

shaded in fig. 1. Then chamfer the edges of your board back and front, starting with the top and bottom edges, and then finishing with the sides. Give a good glasspapering all round, including the edges. At this point, you can either paint and varnish your board, or just varnish it. The choice is yours.

3 Now for your pegs. First, take your 16 pieces of dowelling, ¾in×³⁄₁₆in (if you are making the board for the hen that lays eggs, then you have only 11 pieces). Round off one end only of each length of dowelling by using a piece of glasspaper. The finished dowelling is shown in fig. 2.

For the bear ziggy-zaggy board, put a little wood glue inside your 16 peg holes. For those making the hen board, you only put wood glue into 11 peg holes – leave the top three and the bottom two holes (shown

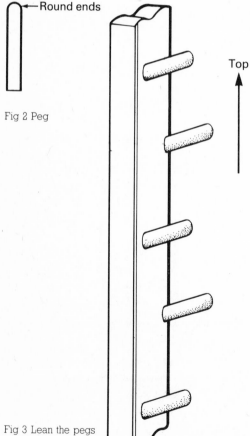

Fig 2 Peg

Fig 3 Lean the pegs gently upwards

Top

in fig. 1c) until later, these are reserved for the hen and egg cup. Take your pegs and push them firmly into the holes that you have glued, until they are flush with the reverse side of your board. Make sure that they are all in an absolutely straight line, and lean gently upwards, at a slight tilt, as shown in fig. 3. These, in turn, will help to keep the figure against the face of the board, when it descends down the board.

For those of you who are making the bear ziggy-zaggy, your board is now complete, except for the figure. The board with the hen and egg cup is waiting for you to make the figures as well.

4 Let us deal with the Teddy bear first, to avoid confusion. Take your tracing paper and trace the outline of the bear, and the surround line as shown in fig. 4. Cut out the box section containing the figure, and pencil the reverse side of the tracing paper. Then place this squarely on to your piece of ⅛in plywood, 3½in×3½in. Don't forget to tape them together to keep them steady. Then transfer the outline of your figure to your piece of plywood. Take your hand fretsaw, and cut out the shape of Teddy bear. Give him a good glasspapering, especially round the edges. Then paint and varnish him. He can be a little brown or black bear, with just his features highlighted, wearing a little collar or scarf around his neck. Or you can choose to dress him in a pair of trousers.

5 Now for the hen that lays eggs. This time, draw yourself a 9in×6in box section on your tracing paper. Trace out your hen, shown in fig. 5, the egg cup, (fig. 6), and the egg itself (fig. 7), by following the layout plan in fig. 8. Keep within your box section, but do not forget your peg-hole positions. Pencil the reverse side of your tracing paper. You can now cut out your box section, and place squarely on to your piece of ⅛in plywood, 9in×6in. Tape both pieces together to hold steady. Transfer your outlines on to your plywood. Next, drill your ³⁄₁₆in holes; three in the hen's body, and two in the egg cup. Now you can cut out all your sections, using your fretsaw. Having done this, you can glasspaper.

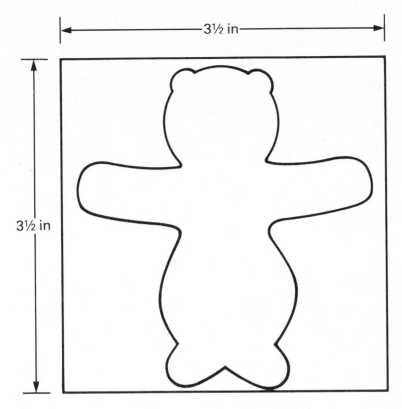

$\leftarrow$——3½ in——$\rightarrow$

3½ in

Fig 4 Bear ziggy-zaggy figure (actual size)

Now place a little wood glue into the peg holes in your hen and the cup. Take your five ³⁄₁₆in lengths of dowelling 1in long, and proceed to push one dowelling into each hole, until they are all flush with the reverse side. Fit the pegs in the hen, as shown in fig. 5A, making sure that the ends of the pegs line up with their respective holes in the board. Let the glue dry thoroughly, and, when all is dry, glasspaper the front of the hen and egg cup. Make sure that the pegs are level with the face of the plywood. Now, you can paint the hen, egg cup and both sides of the egg, if you wish. Then varnish these, when dry.

6 When all is dry, take your board with the eleven pegs, already happily seated, and put a little wood glue into the five last remaining holes. Remember, you should have three at the top, and two at the bottom. Then, gently but firmly, push your hen into the top three holes, and your painted egg cup into the bottom two holes, until flush with

the reverse side. Having done this, you can tie your piece of string through the ⅛in hole at the top of the board, and tie a loop behind. Now to test your toy!

Hang your board up on a nail or affixed screw. Then just drop your bear down the board. And you have a steady Teddy! Just drop your egg behind your hen, and hey-presto, down he comes. On the way down, you can sing either, 'hey little hen, when, when when, will you lay me an egg for my tea?', or 'the bear necessities of life'!

Materials
1 piece ¼in plywood, 3in×18in
16 pieces ³⁄₁₆in dowelling ¾in long (bear board)
11 pieces ³⁄₁₆in dowelling ¾in long
1 piece ⅛in plywood, 3½in×3½in (for bear)
1 piece ⅛in plywood, 9in×6in (for hen, cup and egg)
5 pieces ³⁄₁₆in dowelling 1in long
1 piece string, 6in long × ¹⁄₁₆in thick

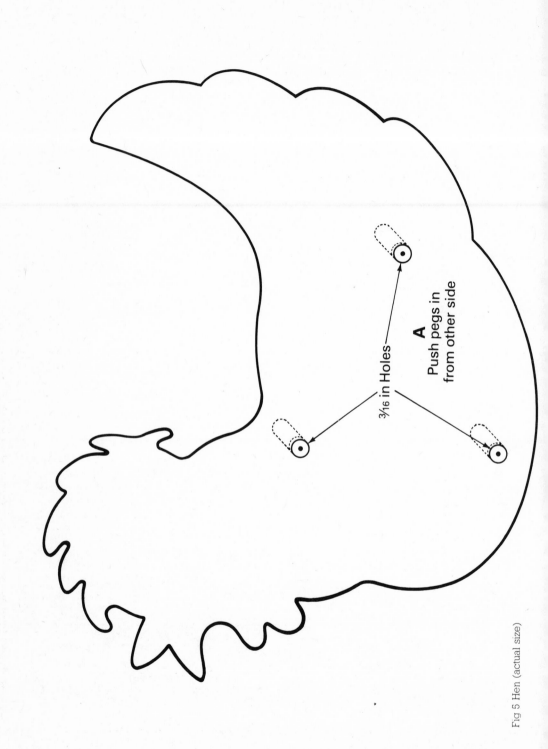

3⁄16 in Holes

A
Push pegs in
from other side

Fig 5 Hen (actual size)

Fig 6 Egg cup (actual size)

¾16 in Holes

Fig 7 Egg (actual size)

9 in

6 in

Fig 8 Hen laying egg layout plan

91

14 The Ladderman

Colour plate 7

This is one of the truly great moving folk toys of all time. We have made vast numbers of different types of laddermen throughout the years, and have found that their appeal is universal; they fascinate just as many adults as children. They are terrific playthings, and utterly irresistible!

The ladderman originated in Bavaria and Czechoslovakia, and has since spread all over the world. Our very first one consisted of painted oblong blocks with contrasting backgrounds on either side; for example, a laughing moon on a background of stars and the smiling sun shining though clouds in a powder blue sky; a mermaid at the bottom of the sea, and a pilot flying his aircraft through the sky; and then we found that a shaped figure was equally effective and simple to make, and we made a Humpty Dumpty figure, soldiers, sailors, bears, clowns, and many others.

Severely handicapped people of all ages take a delight in this toy; all you have to do to make it work is to drop the figure down onto the topmost rung of the ladder – it really doesn't matter whether he goes head or feet first! – and he'll tumble, head over heels, all the way down.

You may think that the ladderman drawing looks really complicated, but don't worry; it's a sophisticated toy, but really easy to make so long as you take your time and don't panic. You'll soon produce a ladderman that will amaze everyone.

This toy begs not to be confined just to the nursery. Many junior and senior executives find it a great aid to both concentration and relaxation. By placing it in a prominent position on their desks, they can then watch the ladderman fall unerringly down his ladder. Who knows just how many great and small decisions have been taken with the aid of this delightful plaything!

Method

1 Take the two square ramin lengths (fig. 1A) and lay them side by side on a flat surface, making sure that the tops are flush together. Sellotape the lengths together.

2 Using a sharp pencil and a set square (see fig. 1B) start marking out the ladder from the top downwards in stages as shown: 1¼in, ⅜in and 2½in, finishing with sections of 3⅝in and ¾in.

3 Mark a centre line in each of the ⅜in sections on the ladder-sides (fig. 2A). Then mark ¹⁄₁₆in on either side of the centre lines (this will produce the ⅜in × ⅛in holes for the rungs). Using a hand or electric drill, drill three ⅛in holes to a depth of ⁵⁄₁₆in in each rung section. To judge the depth accurately, measure ⁵⁄₁₆in from the tip of the drill and bind some sellotape around the drill a few times to make an effective stop.

4 Clean the holes out with a small chisel or a sharp cutting knife to allow a snug fit for the rungs. (*instructions continue on page 98*)

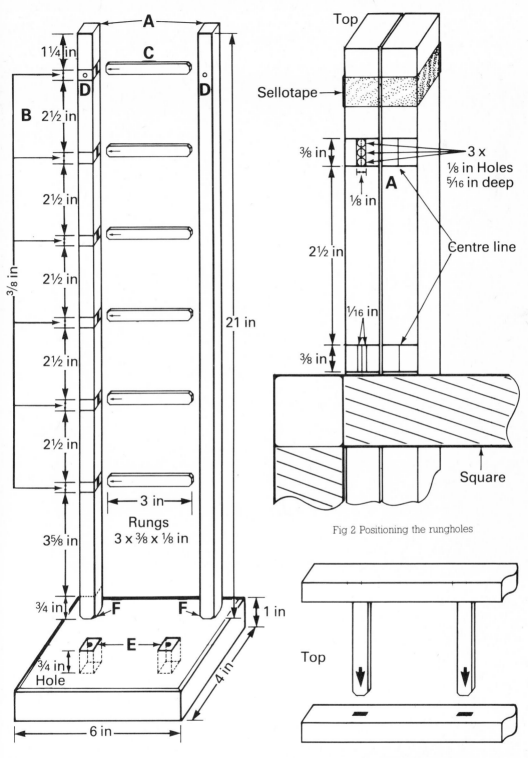

A

C

1¼ in

D   D

B   2½ in

2½ in

3/8 in

2½ in

21 in

2½ in

2½ in

2½ in

←—3 in—→

Rungs
3 x 3/8 x 1/8 in

3⅝ in

¾ in   F   F   1 in

E

¾ in
Hole   4 in

←—— 6 in ——→

Fig 1 Constructing the ladder

Top

Sellotape →

3/8 in   3 x
                  1/8 in Holes
1/8 in   5/16 in deep

2½ in   A

            Centre line
1/16 in

3/8 in

Square

Fig 2 Positioning the rungholes

Top

Fig 3 Tapping the rungs in position

97

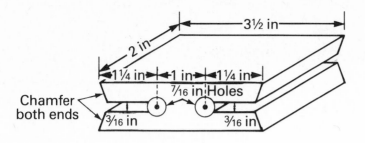

Chamfer
both ends

Fig 4 Marking out the ladderman block

Fig 5 Humpty
Dumpty ladderman
shape

5 Take the six pieces of plywood or ramin (rungs) and chamfer each corner (fig. 1c). This will ensure that the rungs fit into the ladder-sides easily.

6 Dab a little glue inside the rung holes, and gently tap in the six rungs on one side with a small hammer. Place the other ladder-side down flat, and repeat this operation (fig. 3). You can easily guide the rungs home in this way.

7 Using the two moulding pins, pin each side of the topmost rung (fig. 1D).

8 Make the base (see fig. 1) and chamfer the edges. Rest the ladder upright on top of the base, making sure that it is positioned centrally. Mark the position of the ladder on the base as shown in fig. 1E. Using a ½in drill, centre punch and drill two holes to the depth of ¾in.

9 Chamfer the bottom edges of the ladder-sides with a knife or raspblade (fig. 1F). Glue inside the two holes in the base, and tap the ladder home, making sure that it stands square.

10 **The Ladderman.** Mark out your block (fig. 4) and drill two ⁷⁄₁₆in holes right through it, making sure that you do it squarely – don't rush.

11 Using a tenon or hacksaw, cut out two ³⁄₁₆in slots on either side of the block. Chamfer on either side of the block, working inwards to the slots (this will allow the block to slide easily on the ladder rungs). Sandpaper the block, making it as smooth as possible.

12 If you are feeling ambitious, you can mark out, cut and shape a curved figure, using the Humpty Dumpty shape shown in fig. 5, or the soldier figure shown on the jacket, and a fretsaw; but make sure that the block will fall freely down from the top of the rungs to the base.

13 All that is left is to paint the block or figure brightly; varnish the figure, ladder and base, and let them dry thoroughly – and you have made the enchanting ladderman!

Materials
2 pieces ramin, ½in × ½in × 21in
6 pieces plywood or ramin, ³⁄₈in × ⅛in × 3in
two ½in moulding pins
1 piece hardwood, 6in × 4in × 1in (for base)
1 piece hardwood, 3½in × 2in × 1in (for figure)

15 The Jig-dancing Doll
Colour plate 8

The jig-dancing doll, one of our very favourite things, is capable of bringing immense pleasure and amusement to everyone; Anthony's Irish grandfather Graham used to make these many years ago, so we are definitely carrying on a family tradition. The jig doll was not, however, originally conceived as a plaything. It was the stock in trade for hundreds of years of the travelling entertainers who journeyed around Europe; and indeed, many still do so today. No one actually knows who invented them; the Celts of both Wales and Ireland lay strong claim. What we do know is that the dolls are universally popular. I have lost count of the number and types of jig-dancing dolls that we have made, not only for the public at large, but also for amateur and professional folk musicians and singers, magicians, entertainers and buskers, all over the world. You name the country, and there is a pretty good chance that one of our dolls will be throbbing away somewhere out there!

About two hundred years ago, a vast number of people from Europe and Scandinavia upped and emigrated to the United States of America. They shared many attributes. They were enterprising and resourceful, and in the main were skilled in the use of tools. They also took along, together with their few possessions, the jig-dancing doll. Now, the Americans weren't slow in latching on to a brilliant idea such as this one, and promptly began to make their own dolls, called 'clapboard dancers'. 'Dancing Dinah', made about 1800, was made and painted as a Negro lady. Toymaking in the USA developed quite naturally after the settlers had built their own log cabins and made their own furniture. They then whittled and carved toys for their children. The jig-dancing doll was a fine and amusing way of passing a long winter evening for the whole family. And so, the settlers established themselves, and the country grew and prospered, the toymaking industry along with it. It was in the mid 1800s, that the first toymaking firms began to flourish, in Connecticut. There was no

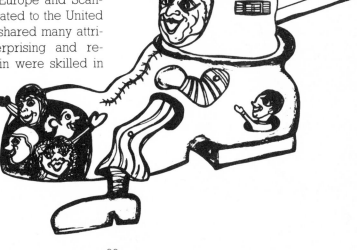

stopping the Americans now. Metal jig dolls were later made that danced on phonographs as the record revolved. Characters that date the period in which they were produced involved Uncle Sam chasing Pancho Villa. Two close relatives of the dolls that we know of are the 'Marionette à la Planchette', which involves two dolls dancing on a board, and the 'Knee Britch Marionette', where the doll is secured to the knee and made to dance from the foot.

To see the doll dance well, in time to music or song or both, is a wonderful thing to experience. In spite of having little technique or musical accomplishments, but having a great deal of chutzpah, my own *pièce de résistance* is singing *à la* George Formby, while I dance the doll, 'leaning on the lamppost'. My individual rendering of this theme has been known to make strong men weep with laughter, but, as Anthony says, 'It is better to make people laugh, than to cry'.

This particular version that we show you how to make is the clown. He is eight inches high, lightweight and strong, and very suitable for the handicapped. We have found that all children love this clown, because they can work it themselves. Everyone, of any age in the family, has a go at dancing the clown. It is ever so easy. Make one and see, and, after making your first jig-dancing doll, you will find that there are other characters you can go on to create. Now's the time to develop your penchant for woodcarving as well. How about making some of the jig-dancing dolls that we have made in the past? There is a Cossack dancer, master of foxhounds, sailor, soldier, Humpty Dumpty, jockey, song-and-dance man, Confederate captain, turkey and duck – the list becomes endless! We even made a pantomime horse, although, for this commission, we experienced a great deal of difficulty in deciding where to insert the dancing stick in his body. Make this jig-dancing doll firstly though, and you, your family and friends are assured of perpetual amusement for years to come.

CLARENCE THE CLOWN
Method

1 The first operation is to make the body of the clown. So, take up your tracing paper, and draw a 3in×7in box section. Then place this on the illustration shown in fig. 1A, and trace out the outline of the body, including the cut-out positions, which eventually will take the body joints shown in fig. 1B, for the legs to fit and pivot on. Now, cut out your box section, with a sharp pair of scissors. Having done this, pencil the reverse side of the tracing paper, and place squarely on to one piece of ¼in plywood; tape together to hold steady. Transfer the outline of the body to your plywood. Next, take your second piece of ¼in plywood and put a little wood glue over the whole top surface, and glue your two pieces of plywood together. Nail together these two pieces at each of the four corners, and leave them to dry.

2 Take your fretsaw, and cut out the body. When you arrive at the cut-out positions for the joints, don't forget to cut to the insides of the lines. Now you have a choice. You can leave the body-piece flat, or you can choose to scallop the sides of the body, as shown in fig. 1. This will give the clown more of a shaped waistline. Also, you can shape his hat, and the cheeks of his face, using a small file. You do not need to shape the back of the doll, as all the attention will be focused on the front.

Having completed this task, you can drill your holes. You need a ⁵⁄₁₆in hole in the centre of the back, to a depth of ⁷⁄₁₆in. The handle will fit into this. One hole for his nose, ³⁄₁₆in, about ¼in deep. Finally, a ¹⁄₁₆in pilot hole for your screws, into each side of the shoulder. Now, give the body-piece a good glasspapering all round.

Next, put a little wood glue into the joint slots, and then push the body joints firmly all the way to the top, making sure that they are flush with the body on both sides. If not, just wait until the glue has dried, and then make them flush by using a file and glasspaper, shown in fig. 1c, showing body joints in position. And then, last but not least, take a piece of ³⁄₁₆in scrap dowelling about ½in long, and push this into the nose hole of the face, after glueing one end of it. (You can also shape the nose, by using a piece of glasspaper against the dowelling end. Don't be too hard on his nose; too much rubbing creates a snub nose, and a little judicious rubbing can create a Pinocchio-type nose!) Finally, give the whole body a final rub-down with glasspaper, and then place your body-piece to one side, for the moment.

3 Now for the dancing doll's arms. Trace the arms, complete with screw holes and box, as shown in fig. 2, and then cut out your box section. Pencil the reverse side of the tracing paper, taping this to your ⅛in plywood, 1¾in×3in. Then transfer this outline to your plywood. Drill the ⅛in screw holes, and countersink. Proceed to cut out the arms; then glasspaper.

4 See fig. 3A. Trace out the clown's boots (top view), and transfer the outline to your 1½in×1½in×½in piece of hardwood. Drill your ³⁄₁₆in hole in each boot, to a depth of ⅜in. Take your hand fretsaw, and cut out the shapes marked. Now mark as shown in fig. 3A, side view, the side shapes of the boots. You should be able to cope with this freehand. Then cut out these shapes, and glasspaper.

Fig. 3B – your 2 pieces of dowelling, ³⁄₁₆in×1½in long. These parts are what we call the ankles. To fit these, just put a little wood glue inside the holes of the boots, and firmly push the ankles into the boots. Then, put these to one side.

Fig. 3C. Take your 1¾in×¾in×⅛in plywood, and draw two ¾in diameter circles. These are for the trouser turn-ups. Next, drill a ³⁄₁₆in hole through the centre of each circle. Don't forget to rest your piece of plywood on to some scrap wood when doing this, as it makes this operation easier to perform. Now, cut out your marked circles, and glasspaper around the edges (we don't want our clown to have tatty trousers). Push the circles of the trouser-tops down over the ankles of the clown.

Fig 1 Jig-dancing doll body and body joint sections; 1C shows how to assemble body and body joints

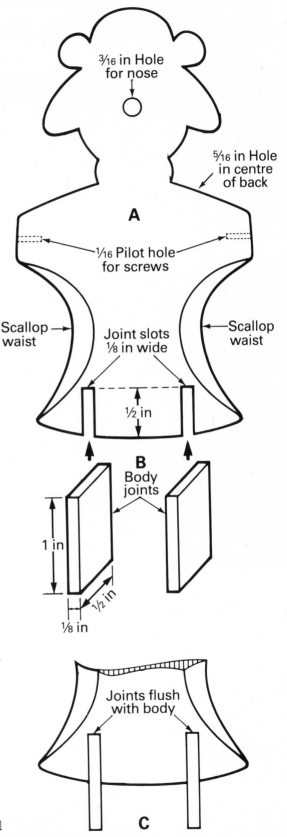

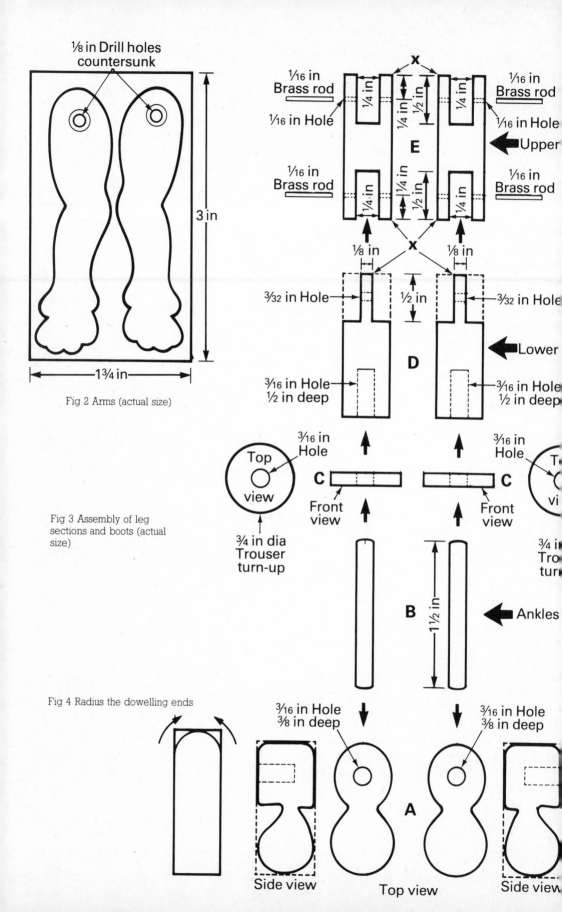

⅛ in Drill holes countersunk

3 in

1¾ in

Fig 2 Arms (actual size)

X

1/16 in Brass rod
1/16 in Hole
¼ in
¼ in
½ in
¼ in
1/16 in Brass rod
1/16 in Hole
Upper

E

1/16 in Brass rod
1/16 in Hole
¼ in
¼ in
½ in
¼ in
1/16 in Brass rod
1/16 in Hole

X

⅛ in
⅛ in

3/32 in Hole
½ in
3/32 in Hole

D

Lower

3/16 in Hole ½ in deep
3/16 in Hole ½ in deep

Fig 3 Assembly of leg sections and boots (actual size)

3/16 in Hole
Top view
¾ in dia Trouser turn-up

C
Front view

C
Front view

3/16 in Hole
T
vi
¾ i
Tro
tur

B

1½ in

Ankles

Fig 4 Radius the dowelling ends

3/16 in Hole
⅜ in deep
3/16 in Hole
⅜ in deep

A

Side view
Top view
Side view

Fig. 3D. First, in two pieces of ½in dowelling, 1½in long, drill a ³⁄₁₆in hole to a depth of ½in. Then mark out your joints, and cut out as illustrated. These will be the lower legs of the doll.

Fig. 3E. Take your two remaining pieces ½in dowelling, 1½in long, mark out, and then cut out the joint sections, as illustrated. 5 Next, radius the ends of the dowellings, marked as x on figs. 3D, and 3E. Then, using a file, gently file a radius; work towards the middle, as shown in fig. 4. This will then prevent your splitting the dowelling ends. Having done this, give the legs a good glasspapering, and pay special attention to ensuring smooth joints.

6 Mark out your two ¹⁄₁₆in hinge pin holes in the two upper legs, as shown in fig. 3E, ¼in inwards from each end on one side of the leg only. Then drill a ¹⁄₁₆in hole centrally through the joint, and out the other side. Don't be tempted to take a short cut when doing this particular job, and drill a hole from each side in to your joint. If you do, the holes will be out of line and out of true, and you will find it jolly difficult to knock in your hinge pin. You could also split the dowelling as well, so stick to the way that we have shown, and all will be well! Clean out the burrs from all joints, using a piece of glasspaper.

7 Now to drill your hinge pin holes in the lower legs. Push the lower-leg joints into the upper-leg joints, as shown in fig. 5A. Then mark the position of your ¹⁄₁₆in holes in the upper legs on the lower joints of the legs.

Then take these apart and drill a ³⁄₃₂in hole in the lower legs at the point shown in fig. 5B, immediately above your central mark. This will then allow plenty of clearance when the legs begin their dancing. Sandpaper away any remaining drill burrs.

8 Assembly time again. See figs 3D and 3E. All you have to do is to push the lower-leg joint into the upper-leg joint. Then take one of your ¹⁄₁₆in brass rods, and file a small point at one end. Push this into the hole (starting from the side that you drilled) and, very carefully, knock in your hinge pin through the joint until it becomes level with the opposite side. File level with the leg any bit of protruding brass rod. After identical treatment to the second leg, glasspaper them both.

9 Now you can assemble the legs to the body. Make sure that the joints on the body are the same length as the depth of the joints in the legs. If they are not, then just trim the body joints to match. When you have done this, you can now radius off the body joints, as described in instruction no. 5. Then assemble the legs to the body, using the same procedure as described in instruction nos. 7 and 8.

10 Finally, put a little wood glue around the inside of the holes in the lower legs. Then, in turn, push the ankles (into which you have already glued the boots, and placed the trouser turn-ups) into each hole. Glue around the lower edge of the legs, and push the trouser turn-ups up into position. Do make sure that the boots are facing the front,

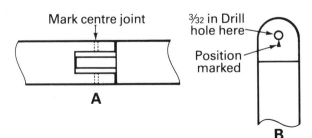

Mark centre joint

A

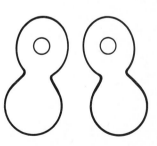

³⁄₃₂ in Drill hole here

Position marked

B

Fig 5 Marking and drilling the hinge bar hole

Fig 6 Position of boots when fitted to legs

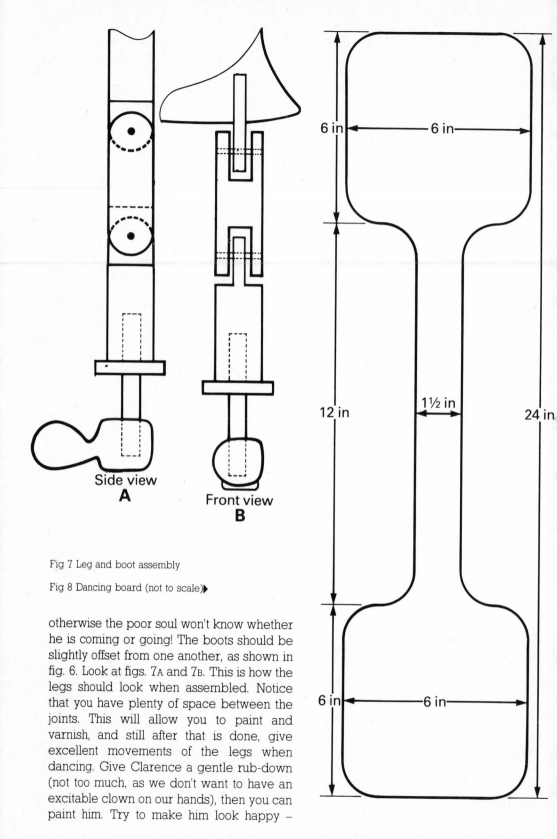

Fig 7 Leg and boot assembly

Fig 8 Dancing board (not to scale)▶

Side view
A

Front view
B

otherwise the poor soul won't know whether he is coming or going! The boots should be slightly offset from one another, as shown in fig. 6. Look at figs. 7A and 7B. This is how the legs should look when assembled. Notice that you have plenty of space between the joints. This will allow you to paint and varnish, and still after that is done, give excellent movements of the legs when dancing. Give Clarence a gentle rub-down (not too much, as we don't want to have an excitable clown on our hands), then you can paint him. Try to make him look happy –

give him a zany expression, or a silly smile, and bright. Don't forget his arms, or the tip of his nose. And then, when you have painted him all over – except for the soles of his feet – you can varnish him. To assemble the arms, firstly ensure that the holes in the arms are clear of all paint and varnish, as otherwise this will impede his swinging along. Then, take your brass screws, and loosely screw the arms to his body.

You now have to make his stage – the dancing board – on which he will perform, *à la* Fred Astaire. This is extremely simple. All that you have to do is to take your last piece of ⅛in plywood, 6in×24in, and mark out as shown in fig. 8. Cut out the dancing board, and give it a good sandpapering. Pay special attention to the edges, for don't forget that you have to sit on one end of the board, and you do want to be comfortable when you do this! And now, just varnish the board. Then take your ⁵⁄₁₆in length of dowelling, 12in long. Pick up your pencil sharpener, and round off the edges of this.

Push the stick into Clarence's back. Sit on one end of your board on a hard chair. Hold the doll's feet about ⅛in above the dancing board. Get your fiddle tuned up, and off we go with a lively jig. Tap the board in rhythm with your music, and the board will spring up and down. And away he dances! You will have all the children, and all the members of your family – no matter what age – all queuing up to have a go! Now, aren't you glad you made him, and isn't he worth while? A veritable treasure? Of course he is!

Materials

2 pieces ¼in plywood, 2¾in×4¾in
2 pieces ⅛in plywood, 1in×½in
1 piece ³⁄₁₆in dowelling, approx. ½in long
1 piece ⅛in plywood, 1¾in×3in
1 piece hardwood, 1½in×1½in×½in
2 lengths ³⁄₁₆in dowelling 1½in long
1 piece ⅛in plywood, 1¾in×¾in
4 lengths ½in dowelling 1½in long
4 brass rods, ¹⁄₁₆in×½in in long
2 countersunk brass woodscrews ¾in size 4s
1 piece ⅛in plywood, 6in×24in
1 length ⁵⁄₁₆in dowelling 12in long

'Serenading the Moon'

Carving is an ancient and universal craft. For thousands of years, men have cut and worked many and varied materials, which included gold and marble, stone, jade and ivory. Woodcarving too, is old. Treen, a folksy word of Saxon origin, literally means 'of the tree'. The oldest wood of all that remains in regular use is oak, because of its hardness, strength and durability. Another type of wood, which even the Romans worked, is boxwood. Mahogany, used mainly for furniture, was a comparitive newcomer, not being worked until the sixteenth century onwards. The best place to see the work of the medieval wood-carvers, the *crème de la crème*, is in many old English churches, where the bench ends of wooden pews testify to the enduring greatness of their art. Here, you may find real people and characters, carved in relief in the wood. They are so very true to life that, except for the mode of dress, they could be our contemporaries. The chutzpah and liveliness of these friezes are extra-ordinary, which proves that the master woodcarvers of those days were blessed with a strong vein of humour.

We have a friend who is a woodcarver. His workshop holds over three hundred tools, including outside and inside knives, gouges and hooking knives, and many others, most of whose names we could not begin to pronounce. He specializes in figurations, reliefs, mouldings and recesses, and incisions. What I am leading up to is this: for 'Serenading the Moon' you need to have no knowledge of woodcarving, whatsoever.

Not too many moons ago, we used to be really poor, even poorer than we are now. It was then when Anthony saw a picture in a book of 'Serenading the Moon'. This was originally a working automata of 'Pierrot serenading the moon', created by that genius of the last century, Vichy. His piece also incorporated a musical movement, which you may also like to attempt later. Anthony took an immediate fancy to this piece. He thought that it would make the most terrific jig-dancing doll, as well as providing us with endless ideas for accompanying songs. 'By the light of the silvery moon', 'Moon River', and 'the moon is shining bright across the Potomac', etc. Anthony didn't have any access then to a professional set of woodworking tools, we had little money and knew nothing of the correct kinds of wood to use for carving, but none of these things deterred him. He set to, and with the aid of only one piece of laminated birch ply, one blunt chisel, two rasp blades, assorted files and one sharpened screwdriver, he created his own version of 'Serenading the Moon'. This piece has been widely recognised as pretty good for a newcomer to crafts. Since its creation, it has figured in various exhibitions and lectures all over the place, down through the years.

It is, in fact, very easy to make. We think that this piece could be a project for the amateur woodworker, fretsaw worker and artist. It can also be developed easily as a multiple project to encompass different crafts. As it is our last piece in this book, and slightly more complex than any of the other toys that we have shown you how to make, we have deliberately placed it last – as a grand finale. The painting is easy, but when you come to paint the eyes of the moon, which are on a sloping surface, do make sure that you have a steady hand, otherwise the moon will look as if he is either cross-eyed or has been imbibing a little more than is good for him.

Having mastered this little piece, you could also go on to create 'the old woman who lives in a shoe', and after that, try something just that little bit harder.

There was an Old Woman

There was an old woman who lived in a shoe,
She had so many children she didn't know what to do.
She gave them some broth without any bread,
And whipped them all soundly and sent them to bed.

(Traditional)

Method

1 At last, you have reached your final project in the book – the carved moon. Now, you don't have to worry; its easy to make. If I can make one, then so can you! Before you actually start work, you are going to need eight pieces of moon. To achieve this, take your piece of ¼in plywood, 9½in × 48in. Starting from one end, draw yourself a grid, with each square representing 1in. Then, following the illustration in fig. 1, draw your moon to scale. Next, cut out the moon, using your hand fretsaw. Using your cut-out moon as a pattern, mark out and cut your remaining seven shapes, using your fretsaw. Now take two sections of your moon, and on one piece, spread a little wood glue over the whole of the top surface, and then glue the two sections together. Make sure that you keep all your edges level. When these are dry, you can glue your third section into place, to the two pieces already glued. Then leave to dry, and continue this until all the sections are glued together; finishing with a moon 2in thick.

2 Now before you start hacking away at the moon, first drill the ¹⁄₁₆in pilot holes for your wood screws, on each side of the moon at the positions shown in fig. 1A, to about ½in deep. Next, drill a ³⁄₈in hole to a depth of 1in shown in fig. 1B, into the back of the moon.

3 Now comes the easy bit – the actual carving. The tools that I used to make this with have all been mentioned in the introductory section. The half-round rasp was used to form the shapes of the crescent of the moon, and also the platform for Pierrot. For 'smoothing off', I used the flat rasp blade, also the files. The chisel I used mainly for shaping the face. I also filed down a small screwdriver to make a sharp edge, and used this to carve inside all the corners. I used the craft knife for trimming away excess wood, and I also used sheets of glasspaper, which is a very good medium for shaping, as well as for smoothing.

Before you start, study the photograph of the shape of the moon, and just follow the step-by-step basic instructions. The shape and style (*instructions continue on page 110*)

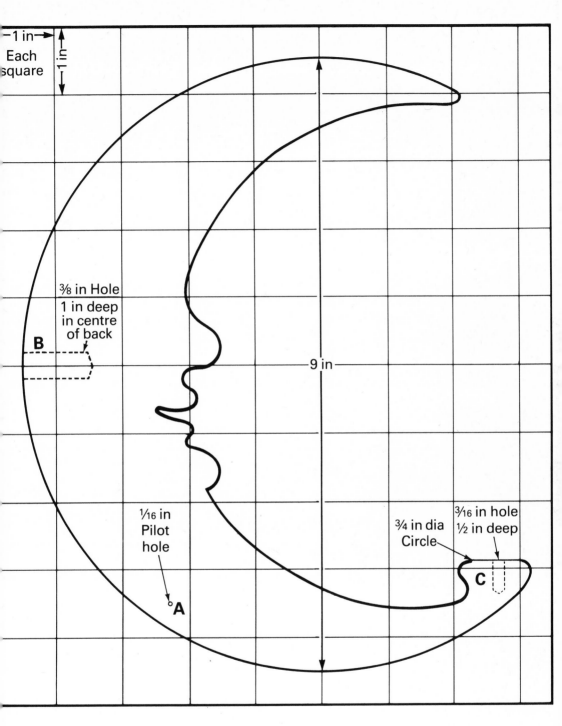

—1 in→
Each square

1 in

⅜ in Hole
1 in deep
in centre
of back

B

9 in

1/16 in
Pilot
hole

¾ in dia
Circle

3/16 in hole
½ in deep

C

A

Fig 1 The moon (not to scale)

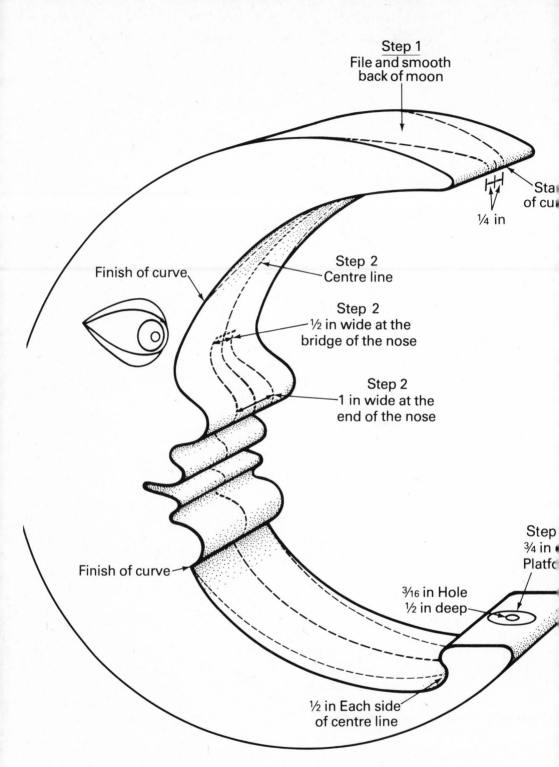

Step 1
File and smooth
back of moon

Sta[...]
of cu[...]

¼ in

Finish of curve

Step 2
Centre line

Step 2
½ in wide at the
bridge of the nose

Step 2
1 in wide at the
end of the nose

Step [...]
¾ in [...]
Platf[...]

³⁄₁₆ in Hole
½ in deep

Finish of curve

½ in Each side
of centre line

Fig 2 Marking out positions of eyes, nose and platform

108

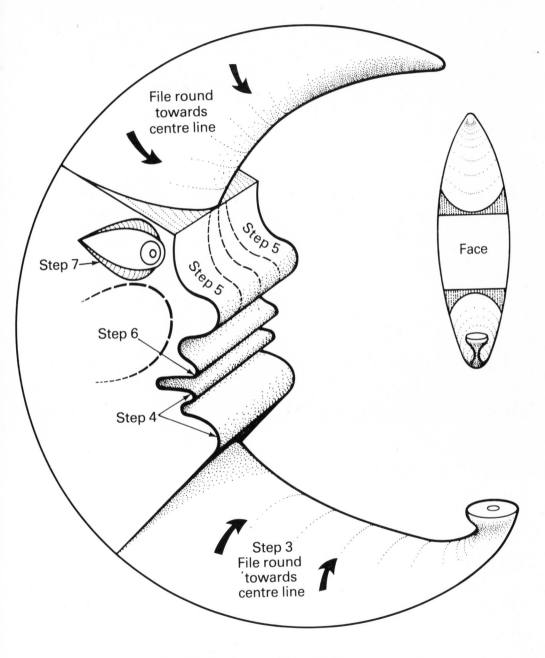

Fig 3 Carving the moon: side and front views

of the face we leave entirely in your capable hands, for carving and whittling away at wood is a very personal and individual medium. Just take your time; this is the main criteria, and only take away a small amount of wood at a time, each step of the way. Remember that you cannot put back that which you have taken off, but you can always trim a little more wood away, if you need to. Also, keep checking both sides of the face as you chip and file, to ensure that both sides of the moon look alike. We don't guarantee that each side will be exactly alike – that would be to achieve perfection. As you work at this, it will amaze you to find that slowly, but surely, everything will fall into place.

Step 1. File or plane the back of the moon smooth and flat.

Step 2. Shown in fig. 2. Draw a centre line from the top of the crescent of the moon right down through to the platform at the lower end of the moon. Then, measure the width of the nose, 1in at the lower end, to ½in at the bridge of the nose. Mark the position and design of the eyes, with top and bottom lids. Finally, mark out a ¾in diameter circle on the top of the platform for Pierrot to sit upon, and here drill a ³⁄₁₆in hole centrally to a depth of ½in. Finally, draw a curve on each side of the crescents of the moon, as shown in fig. 2, starting with the top of the crescent, ¼in each side of your centre line, and finishing with the line above the eye. Then do the same with the lower crescent, measuring ½in each side of your centre line below the platform, finishing just below the chin.

Step 3. First, cut out the curves that you have just marked, by using your hand fretsaw. And then shape these. Shape the top and lower crescents, shown in fig. 3, and also the platform. When doing this, start from just below the chin, downwards towards your platform, and from just above the eyes and upwards, always filing towards the centre line. This stage can be completed before you begin on the actual face of the moon.

Step 4. Round and shape the chin and the lower lip.

Step 5. Carve out and shape the nose, down to the cheeks.

Step 6. Shape the upper lip and also the cheeks.

Step 7. Carefully cut out the shape of the eyes. (If you take too much wood away on one eye, you can, as a last resort, always fit an eye-patch!) Also, cut the eyelids, top and bottom. If you want to put bags under his eyes, then carve bags – after all, he does stay out all night!

And that is that! Just keep on until you are completely satisfied with the shape of the face. And, once you are satisfied – stop immediately! Then, make sure finally that every part of the moon is absolutely smooth. Use plenty of glasspaper for this, and finish him off with a very fine glasspapering. This will then show off the design and the shapes of your laminated plywood.

4 Now, paint the eyes, slowly and steadily, and the lips. Varnish the moon.

5 For the last time, take your tracing paper and draw yourself a 5½in × 3½in box section. Trace the outline of Pierrot, shown in fig. 4, who will serenade the moon. Keep within the lines. Next, cut out your box section, and place squarely on your piece of ¼in plywood, 5½in × 3½in, and tape both together. Transfer the outline on to your plywood.

6 Take up your fretsaw, and cut out the shape of the figure. Next, drill a ³⁄₁₆in hole, ½in deep at the position shown in fig. 4A. Put a little wood glue inside the hole, and take up your length of ³⁄₁₆in dowelling, 1in long. Push this firmly into the hole, for this is the peg that holds Pierrot on to the platform of the moon. Now you can glasspaper Pierrot. Then paint him, playing his mandolin. If you cannot manage to paint him well, showing his hands holding his instrument, you can always change his instrument into an oar, so that he appears to be paddling his own canoe. When you have finished painting him, varnish the figure.

7. Now for the legs. Take your four lengths of ⁵⁄₈in dowelling, 2in long, for the legs; two lengths of ⁵⁄₁₆in dowelling, 1¼in long, for the ankles; one piece of hardwood, 2¼in ×

Fig 4 Pierrot (actual size)

A

3/16 in Hole
1/2 in deep

1 in

3/16 in

2½in × 1in to make his boots; and your two 1/16in brass rods for the hinge pins. To make and assemble the legs, follow the same procedure for making the clown's legs, in the previous section. See fig. 3 and instructions 6 to 10 (page 103). But follow the measurements in fig. 5 (page 112). The only difference in the legs is that you have no turn-ups of the trousers to attend to; also the holes in the tops of the legs are bigger. In these you should drill an ⅛in hole, and a 5/16in hole into this ⅛in hole to a depth of

5/16in (see fig. 5A); this then allows room when you screw the legs to the body to fit a capping dowel, so as to hide the screws. It also makes a neater job of work too.

8 Now you can paint the legs and varnish them.

9 When all is dry, loosely screw the legs to the body. Make sure that the 5/16in holes face outwards, and that the boots face forwards. Cut two small pieces of 5/16in dowelling, about ⅛in thick, and push these into the two screw holes, until they become flush with

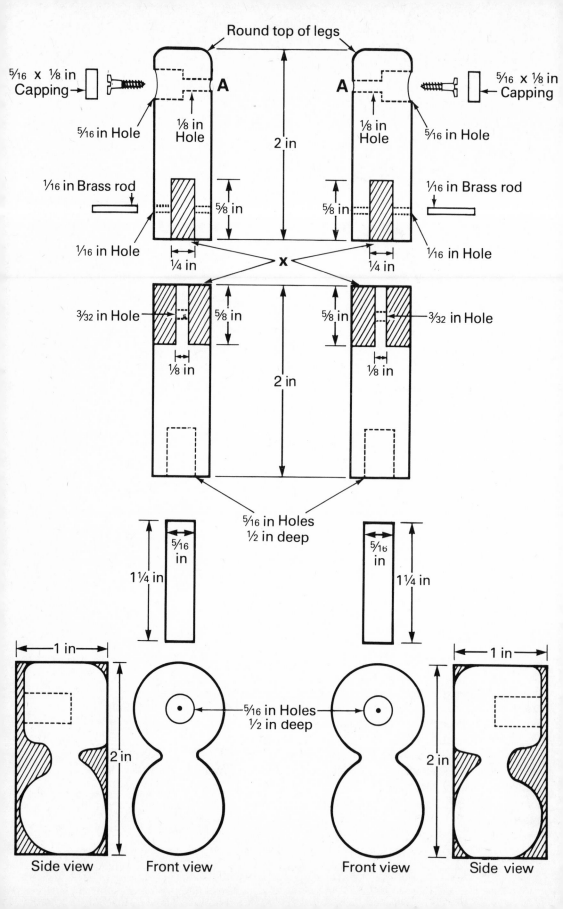

Round top of legs

5/16 x 1/8 in Capping →

5/16 in Hole

1/8 in Hole

A

A

1/8 in Hole

5/16 in Hole

5/16 x 1/8 in Capping

1/16 in Brass rod

1/16 in Hole

5/8 in

2 in

5/8 in

1/16 in Brass rod

1/16 in Hole

1/4 in

X

1/4 in

3/32 in Hole →

5/8 in

5/8 in

← 3/32 in Hole

1/8 in

2 in

1/8 in

5/16 in Holes 1/2 in deep

5/16 in

1 1/4 in

5/16 in

1 1/4 in

1 in

2 in

5/16 in Holes 1/2 in deep

1 in

2 in

Side view

Front view

Front view

Side view

the leg (fig. 5A). Paint these the same colour as you have painted the legs.

10 Now for the final assembly. Put a little wood glue around the hole in the platform of the moon. Gently push Pierrot's peg firmly into the hole. Take your length of ⅜in dowelling, 16in long, and, with your pencil sharpener, just trim both ends of this. Push the dowelling into the moon's back.

11 Now, all you have to do is to make your doll's dancing board, the same shape as the clown's board (shown in fig. 8, previous section.) Take your last piece of ¼in plywood, 8in×30in. Start with a centre line, and now measure from each end, 8in inwards. Then the centre piece of the board will be 2in wide. Don't forget to radius the corners of this. Then glasspaper all round, and varnish the board.

You operate the working of the moon in exactly the same way as you do the clown. If you think that your creation is too good to be played with, then you can put him in a glass case, and keep him as a family heirloom. One of our customers did this with one of the dancing dolls that we made for him! On the other hand, now that you have made him – use him to give you and yours much pleasure for years and years to come. To paraphrase Neil Armstrong, the moon that you have created is capable of giant leaps and dances for mankind! Have fun!

Materials
1 piece ¼in plywood, 9½in×48in moon
1 piece ¼in plywood, 5½in×3½in Pierrot
1 length ³⁄₁₆in dowelling 1in long
4 lengths ⅝in dowelling 2in long
2 lengths ⁵⁄₁₆in dowelling 1¼in long
1 piece hardwood 2¼in×2½in×1in
2 lengths ¹⁄₁₆in brass rod ⅝in long
2 countersunk brass wood screws ¾in × size 4S
2 small pieces dowelling, ⁵⁄₁₆in×⅛in
1 length ⅜in dowelling 16in long
1 piece ¼in plywood, 8in×30in

Fig 5 Assembly of leg sections and boot (actual size)

Postscript

'Big oaks from little acorns grow'.

Now that you have made this exciting selection of moving folk toys, you may be further inspired to develop more ideas, and thus join the ranks of those brilliant innovators of the past. They began, as did we all, with just a few simple concepts – and just look at what has been achieved up to now. For example, from the sight of flying birds, and the accompanying itching curiosity as to how to get up there and join them, came, firstly, the kite; then artificial wings (you didn't really think that the legend of Daedalus was all fantasy, did you?), and mechanical and clockwork birds that flew aloft; on to Leonardo da Vinci's sketches for a working autogyro (the forerunner of the modern helicopter); then the Wright brothers, and their magnificent *Kitty Hawk*, followed by Wernher von Braun's rockets; the satellite, and satellite communications, and the first landing on the moon; and the Challenger flights, and the future plans to propel space vehicles equipped with large sails across the heavens, by solar winds. . . . Everyone has to begin somewhere.

From the simple arm and body movements of toys came working automata, sophisticated enough to paint and draw pictures and to play chess; and robots, computors and artificial limbs. . . .

With the basic knowledge that you have acquired, you can now go on and take an interest in developing some, or all of the following toys and playthings that we know of. Toys powered by water, sand, weights, wheels, levers, wind and electricity; and heat and gravity, clockwork, magnets, and even coin-operated mechanisms. All can be created from wood. On the journey there, your knowledge of mathematics, art, physics, and many other fascinating disciplines, will improve in leaps and bounds! We hope that we have succeeded in arousing your interest in the marvellous world of moving wooden folk toys.

Anthony and Judy Peduzzi
The Lizard, Cornwall

Acknowledgements

We would like to express our gratitude to three lovely people for making this book possible: Derek and Jo Godfrey, and George Carey.

We would also like to thank the public – at large; all the thousands of men, women and children from all over the world, who have immeasurably enriched our lives.

Especially, we are deeply indebted to hundreds of people who went out of their way to explain, and to sketch and, in many cases, to show us their old moving folk toys.

Thank you all for giving us so many good ideas.

Index

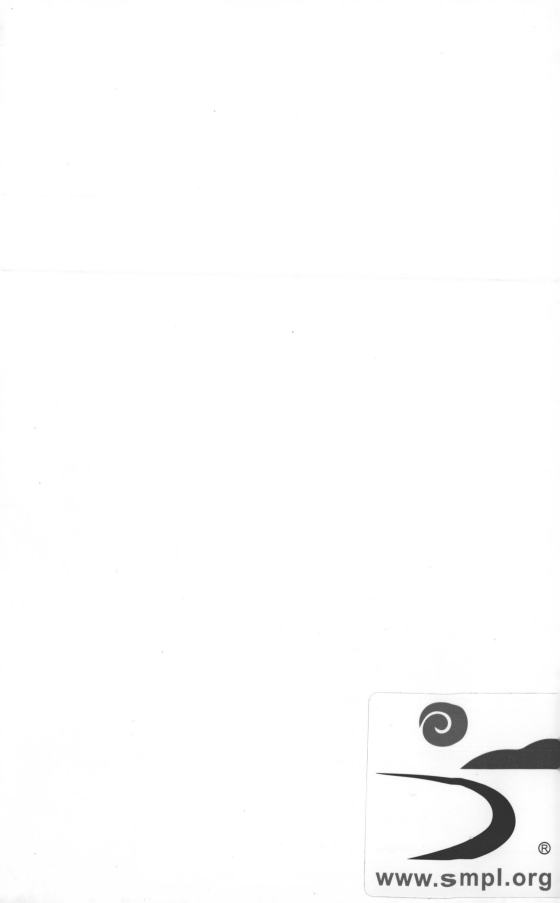

www.smpl.org